YORK NOTES

D0231131

MACBETH

WILLIAM SHAKESPEARE

NOTES BY JAMES SALE
REVISED BY ALISON POWELL

PEARSON

YORK PRESS

YORK PRESS
322 Old Brompton Road, London SW5 9JH

PEARSON EDUCATION LIMITED
Edinburgh Gate, Harlow,
Essex CM20 2JE, United Kingdom
Associated companies, branches and representatives throughout the world

First published 1997
New editions 2002 and 2010
This new and fully revised edition 2015

14

ISBN 978–1–4479–8220–3

Illustrations by Sue Woollatt, and Moreno Chiacchiera (page 61 only)
Phototypeset by DTP Media
Printed in Slovakia

Photo credits: Victor Kunz/Shutterstock for page 8 middle / mubus7/ Shutterstock for page 9 top / Igor Zh./Shutterstock for page 10 middle / Vasiliy Koval/Shutterstock for page 12 bottom / Mirelle/Shutterstock for page 15 bottom / Dani Simmonds/Shutterstock for page 17 top / RTimages/ Shutterstock for page 18 top / Eric Isselee/Shutterstock for page 22 bottom / FXQuadro/Shutterstock for page 23 bottom / apidach.jsw/Shutterstock for page 24 bottom / Auhustinovich/Shutterstock for page 25 bottom / BrAt82/ Shutterstock for page 26 bottom / katalinks/Shutterstock for page 28 bottom / rhfletcher/Shutterstock for page 35 bottom / Sashkin/Shutterstock for page 36 middle / Scotshot/Shutterstock for page 39 / Valentin Valkov/Shutterstock for page 40 middle / Philip Bird LRPSCPAGB/Shutterstock for page 43 bottom / Razumovskaya Marina Nikolaevna/Shutterstock for page 47 middle / TaraPatta/ Shutterstock for page 49 bottom / aaltair/Shutterstock for page 49 top / daseaford/Shutterstock for page 52 bottom / Shutter_M/Shutterstock for page 55 bottom / albund/Shutterstock for page 57 bottom / burnell/Shutterstock for page 58 middle / Pavel Shloyko/Shutterstock for page 59 bottom / Mark Graves/Shutterstock for page 60 bottom / Andrey Burmakin/Shutterstock for page 63 / Franck Boston/Shutterstock for page 64 middle / Sergej Razvodovskij/ Shutterstock for page 65 top / Eric Isselee/Shutterstock for page 66 middle / oriontrail/Shutterstock for page 67 top / Aksenova Natalya/Shutterstock for page 67 bottom / Aleksey Stemmer/Shutterstock for page 68 middle / wavebreakmedia/Shutterstock for page 79 middle

CONTENTS

PART ONE:
GETTING STARTED

Preparing for assessment..5

How to use your York Notes Study Guide 6

PART TWO:
PLOT AND ACTION

Plot summary..8

Act I..10

Act II...18

Act III..23

Act IV...30

Act V...34

Progress and revision check...42

PART THREE:
CHARACTERS

Who's who?...44

King Duncan..45

Macbeth...46

Lady Macbeth...48

Banquo 50

Macduff 51

The witches...52

Malcolm, Lady Macduff and Ross..53

Progress and revision check...54

PART FOUR:
THEMES, CONTEXTS AND SETTINGS

Themes...55

Contexts...59

Settings...60

Progress and revision check.....................................62

PART FIVE:
FORM, STRUCTURE AND LANGUAGE

Form...63

Structure...64

Language..66

Progress and revision check.....................................69

PART SIX:
PROGRESS BOOSTER ★

Understanding the question 70

Planning your answer 70

Responding to writers' effects 72

Using quotations..74

Spelling, punctuation and grammar.........................75

Annotated sample answers.......................................76

Practice task and further questions 82

PART SEVEN:
FURTHER STUDY AND ANSWERS

Literary terms..83

Checkpoint answers...84

Progress and Revision check answers 85

Mark scheme 88

PREPARING FOR ASSESSMENT

HOW WILL I BE ASSESSED ON MY WORK ON *MACBETH?*

All exam boards are different but whichever course you are following, your work will be examined through these four Assessment Objectives:

Assessment Objectives	Wording	Worth thinking about ...
AO1	Read, understand and respond to texts. Students should be able to: • maintain a critical style and develop an informed personal response • use textual references, including quotations, to support and illustrate interpretations.	• How well do I know what happens, what people say, do etc? • What do *I* think about the key ideas in the play? • How can I support my viewpoint in a really convincing way? • What are the best quotations to use and when should I use them?
AO2	Analyse the language, form and structure used by a writer to create meanings and effects, using relevant subject terminology where appropriate.	• What specific things does the writer 'do'? What choices has Shakespeare made (why this particular word, phrase or speech here? Why does this event happen at this point?) • What effects do these choices create – suspense? Ironic laughter? Reflective mood?
AO3	Show understanding of the relationships between texts and the contexts in which they were written.	• What can I learn about society from the play? (What does it tell me about witchcraft in Shakespeare's day, for example?) • What was society like in Shakespeare's time? Can I see it reflected in the story?
AO4	Use a range of vocabulary and sentence structures for clarity, purpose and effect, with accurate spelling and punctuation.	• How accurately and clearly do I write? • Are there small errors of grammar, spelling and punctuation I can get rid of?

Look out for the Assessment Objective labels throughout your York Notes Study Guide – these will help to focus your study and revision!

The text used in this Study Guide is the Penguin Shakespeare edition, 2005.

HOW TO USE YOUR YORK NOTES STUDY GUIDE

You are probably wondering what is the best and most efficient way to use your York Notes Study Guide on *Macbeth*. Here are three possibilities:

A **step-by-step** study and revision guide	A **'dip-in' support** when you need it	A **revision guide** after you have finished the play
Step 1: Read Part Two as you read the play as a companion to help you study it. **Step 2:** When you need to, turn to Parts Three to Five to focus your learning. **Step 3**: Then, when you have finished use Parts Six and Seven to hone your exam skills, revise and practise for the exam.	Perhaps you know the play quite well, but you want to check your understanding and practise your exam skills? Just look for the section which you think you need most help with and go for it!	You might want to use the Notes after you have finished your study, using Parts Two to Five to check over what you have learned, and then work through Parts Six and Seven in the immediate weeks leading up to your exam.

HOW WILL THE GUIDE HELP YOU STUDY AND REVISE?

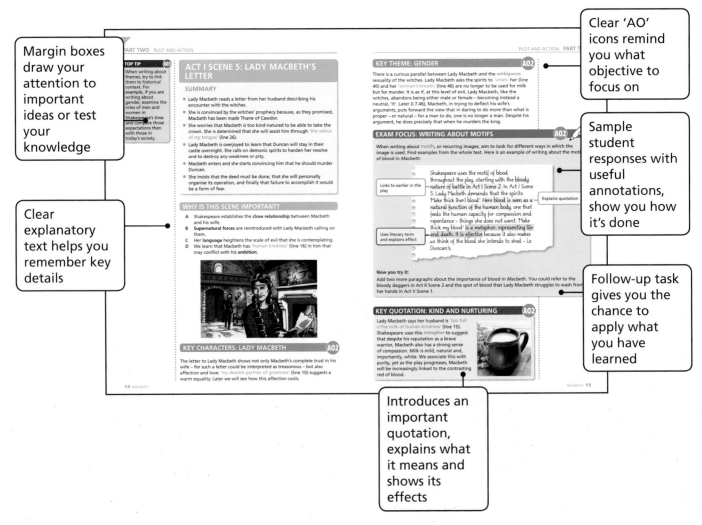

Margin boxes draw your attention to important ideas or test your knowledge

Clear explanatory text helps you remember key details

Clear 'AO' icons remind you what objective to focus on

Sample student responses with useful annotations, show you how it's done

Follow-up task gives you the chance to apply what you have learned

Introduces an important quotation, explains what it means and shows its effects

Extra references to help you focus your revision

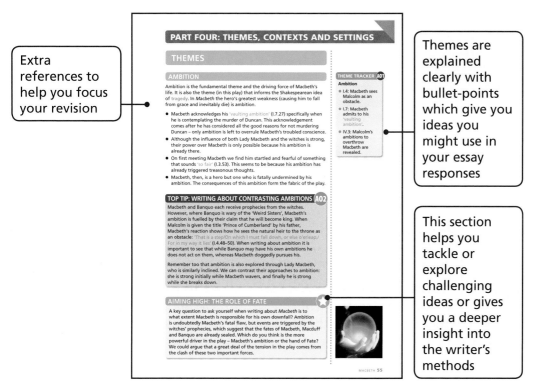

Themes are explained clearly with bullet-points which give you ideas you might use in your essay responses

This section helps you tackle or explore challenging ideas or gives you a deeper insight into the writer's methods

Each key section of the book ends with a **Progress and Revision Check**:

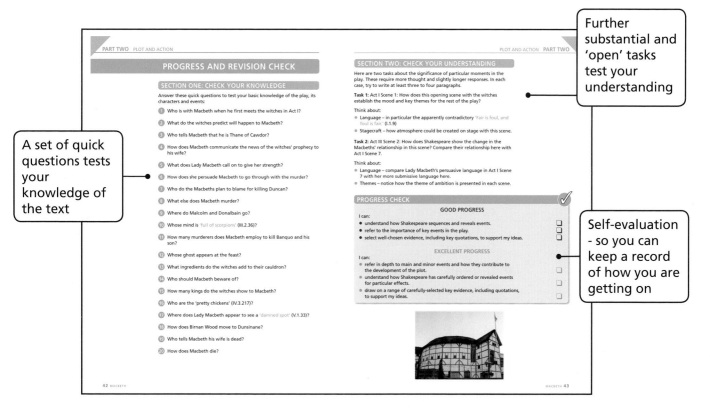

Further substantial and 'open' tasks test your understanding

A set of quick questions tests your knowledge of the text

Self-evaluation - so you can keep a record of how you are getting on

... and don't forget Parts Six and Seven, with advice and practice on **improving your writing skills**:

- Focus on **difficult areas** such as **'context'** and **'inferences'**.
- **Short snippets** of **other students' work** to show you how it's done (or not done!)
- Three, annotated **sample responses** to a task **at different levels**, with **expert comments**, to help you judge your own level.
- **Practice questions**
- **Answer key** with answers to the **Progress and Revision Checks** and **Checkpoint** margin boxes.

Now it's up to you! Don't forget – there's even more help on our website with more sample answers, essay planners and even online tutorials. Go to www.yorknotes.com to find out more.

PLOT SUMMARY: WHAT HAPPENS IN *MACBETH*?

ACT I: PROPHECIES AND PLOTS

- King Duncan plans to reward brave Macbeth with the title Thane of Cawdor for having defeated rebel forces in battle.
- Three witches prophesy that Macbeth will be Thane of Cawdor and King of Scotland.
- Macbeth is officially informed that he has become Thane of Cawdor. He is amazed the witches' prophecy has come true and reveals his hopes for the crown of Scotland.
- Macbeth's wife, Lady Macbeth, shares his ambition and calls on evil spirits to give her the strength to undertake the murder of Duncan.
- Duncan arrives at Macbeth's castle, where he is welcomed.
- When Macbeth arrives home his wife insists on planning the murder.

ACT II: MURDER MOST FOUL

- Worried about the murder he is about to commit, Macbeth sees a vision of a dagger.
- He murders Duncan, although afterwards Lady Macbeth criticises him for being distressed. She helps to cover up the murder and they then go to bed to pretend innocence.
- Macduff, another Thane, finds Duncan murdered and the alarm is sounded.
- Macbeth slays Duncan's guards to cover his crime, but says he did it in fury because they murdered Duncan.
- Duncan's sons, Malcolm and Donalbain, slip away in fear of their lives.
- Macbeth succeeds to the throne but Macduff will not attend Macbeth's coronation.

ACT III: BRUTALITY AND BETRAYAL

- Banquo suspects Macbeth of treachery and Macbeth orders his murder and the murder of Banquo's son, Fleance. Although Banquo is killed, Fleance escapes.
- Banquo's ghost appears at Macbeth's banquet and terrorises Macbeth, whose behaviour indicates his guilt to fellow guests.
- Macbeth, now acting independently of his wife, plans to see the witches again.

- The witches prepare to meet him.
- Macduff flees to the English court, leaving his wife and children behind at his castle.

ACT IV: REVENGE

- Macbeth visits the witches and discovers that he should fear Macduff, but that no man born of a woman can harm him. He also learns that he will never be beaten until Birnan Wood comes to Dunsinane.
- After leaving the witches, Macbeth orders the murder of Macduff's wife and children.
- In England, Malcolm tests the loyalty of Macduff, who has recently arrived there from Scotland.
- Macduff learns of the slaughter of his entire family by murders on Macbeth's orders.
- When Malcolm informs Macduff that England will provide an army under Seyward to defeat Macbeth, Macduff vows personally to kill Macbeth.

ACT V: DOWNFALL OF THE MACBETHS

- The English army marches on Macbeth disguised with branches taken from Birnan Wood. Macbeth fortifies his castle at Dunsinane and prepares for a long siege.
- Macbeth learns his wife has died – apparently by suicide – but he is unconcerned, as his life appears to lack any meaning.
- He is enraged when a messenger tells him that Birnan Wood is coming to Dunsinane.
- He abandons his siege plan and goes out to fight; although his army is losing, nobody seems able to kill Macbeth himself. He meets Macduff, who was born by Caesarean (so not of woman), and Macduff kills Macbeth in single combat.
- Macduff hails Malcolm as King of Scotland and Malcolm invites all to attend his coronation at Scone.

REVISION FOCUS: MAKE SURE YOU KNOW THE PLOT

It is very important you know all the key events in the play so you can make reference to them as needed in the exam. Create a visual reminder chart to make sure you know what happens and when. Either draw images or print them from an internet image search to create a page of collage for each Act. When you have finished, cover the images and see if you can remember each one. Keep testing yourself until you know exactly what happens in each Act.

TOP TIP (A03)

It is useful to know that Shakespeare used real historical figures as the basis for this story: Malcolm reigned as Malcolm III and his son, Duncan, became Duncan II. Consider how this might have been appealing to the royal patron, James I.

ACT I SCENE 1: THREE WITCHES

SUMMARY

- Three witches meet in the middle of a storm.
- They speak in riddles and rhymes, using strange language such as 'hurly-burly' (line 3).
- They are preparing to entice Macbeth 'upon the heath' (line 6).
- A sense of foreboding is created by their choral lines that set up the theme of deception where 'Fair is foul, and foul is fair' (line 9).

WHY IS THIS SCENE IMPORTANT?

A It **immediately** grabs our **attention** with its dramatic nonrealism.

B It raises our sense of **curiosity** and **expectancy**.

C It establishes the importance of **supernatural powers** in the play.

CHECKPOINT 1 **A01**

How does Shakespeare show and interest us in the witches at the beginning of the play?

KEY SETTING: MOOD AND ATMOSPHERE **A02**

The opening scene of the play is brief, but effective in creating an ominous atmosphere. The stage directions ask for *'Thunder and lightning'* and this weather disturbance reflects the evil, disruptive nature of the witches. Shakespeare heightens this atmosphere by starting the scene with a question 'When shall we three meet again?' (line 1). This implies that the witches have prior experience of casting malevolent spells. The air is 'filthy' (line 12) and this also suggests dark deeds are about to happen – the audience's imagination is captured.

KEY CHARACTERS: THE WITCHES **A02**

Shakespeare presents the witches as ambiguous creatures. In Act I Scene 3 they refer to themselves as 'The Weird Sisters' (line 31). Their evil nature is revealed in the final rhyming couplet of this scene where they offer the contrary idea that good is bad and vice versa. Shakespeare suggests that the witches violate the natural order of things by meddling with right and wrong.

KEY CONTEXT: WITCHCRAFT **A03**

In the 1600s it was common to think that witchcraft was real. Shakespeare's patron, King James I, believed in witchcraft, and during his reign practising it was a crime punishable by death. The rhyming language and alliteration of the witches' speech reminds us of a spell and a contemporary audience would have found their contradictory claim that 'fair is foul and foul is fair' particularly unnerving.

ACT I SCENE 2: BRAVE MACBETH

SUMMARY

- King Duncan receives news that the battle against the rebel Macdonwald was evenly balanced, but that Macbeth has killed him.
- The Captain brings news to Duncan that, thanks to Macbeth's and Banquo's courageous actions, his army has won.
- Duncan then declares that the traitorous Thane of Cawdor will be executed and bestows his title and lands on Macbeth as a reward.

WHY IS THIS SCENE IMPORTANT?

A   Shakespeare deepens our **interest** in the character of **Macbeth** by revealing his character through **report**.

B   We switch from the **shadowy** world of witches to the **physical** world of battle.

C   We discover that Macbeth and Banquo have displayed outstanding **bravery**.

D   We find out that Macbeth is to be made **Thane of Cawdor.**

KEY CHARACTER: MACBETH (A01)

Shakespeare has not yet shown us Macbeth, but we have heard about him from the witches in Scene 1 and now from the Captain. While the battle has been violent, their descriptions imply that Macbeth has played a brave and heroic role.

Macbeth is described as 'Valour's minion' (line 19) and 'Bellona's bridegroom' (line 55), meaning bravery's favourite and the husband of war. Duncan praises Macbeth as 'valiant', a 'Worthy gentleman' (line 24) and as 'noble' (line 70).

KEY THEME: BRAVERY (A01)

Macbeth and Banquo are both presented as heroic warriors. It could be argued that both remain brave throughout the play, though of course many of Macbeth's later actions are wicked and cowardly. Notice how appeals to courage always tempt Macbeth – for Macbeth bravery is the essence of being a man.

AIMING HIGH: UNDERSTANDING DRAMATIC IRONY ⭐

Understanding the concept of dramatic irony – where the audience are aware of something that the characters are not – and exploring how Shakespeare uses it is important for attaining higher grades. In *Macbeth*, Shakespeare shows the subtle distinctions between what appears to be and what actually is. In this scene, he uses dramatic irony to achieve this. The execution of the previous Thane of Cawdor allows Duncan to say that he will not deceive him any longer (lines 66–7). However, as the audience learn from Macbeth's asides, the new Thane of Cawdor, is already plotting against the king.

> **TOP TIP** (A01)
>
> Contrast the characters of Banquo and Macbeth – both are brave, but how differently do these characters develop?

ACT I SCENE 3: ALL HAIL, MACBETH!

SUMMARY

- The witches meet as planned, in thunder and rain.
- They greet Macbeth and Banquo and tell them that Macbeth will become both Thane of Cawdor and King of Scotland.
- Macbeth is stunned by these prophecies. Banquo demands the witches tell him of his future too. They predict that he will not be king, but his offspring will.
- The witches vanish and messengers from King Duncan arrive. They report that Macbeth is now Thane of Cawdor.
- Macbeth is astonished by the news and Banquo warns him of danger. Macbeth is preoccupied by thoughts of kingship, which he tries to hide.

WHY IS THIS SCENE IMPORTANT?

A   The witches' prophecies establishes the importance of **fate**.
B   Shakespeare draws significant **contrasts** between Banquo and Macbeth.
C   The theme of **ambition** is introduced when Macbeth becomes preoccupied with thoughts of becoming king.

KEY CHARACTERS: MACBETH AND BANQUO (A02)

Macbeth and Banquo are together when the witches prophesy their future. When Ross arrives and tells Macbeth he has become the Thane of Cawdor both are amazed. We begin to see Macbeth's ambition unfolding through the asides he delivers to the audience. Banquo warns of the danger of trusting such supernatural messages, but Macbeth is lost in his own thoughts, considering the implications.

It is Banquo who thinks the witches are evil: 'What! Can the devil speak true?' (line 108). Macbeth does not. Note how keen Macbeth is to hear more of this 'strange intelligence' (line 77): 'Would they had stayed!' (line 83). In contrast, Banquo's description of the witches is significant in showing us how unnatural they are: they seem to be women but are not.

CHECKPOINT 2 (A01)

Why does Shakespeare have Macbeth wish the witches had stayed?

TOP TIP: WRITING ABOUT IMAGERY (A02)

Notice how Shakespeare begins to develop the imagery of clothing – 'borrowed robes' (line 110) and 'strange garments' (line 146). This is significant because clothing is a powerful image suggesting concealment and disguise: later, Macbeth, as it were, hides behind his clothes of office. Look for this imagery in other, later references.

ACT I SCENE 4: MALCOLM TO BE KING

SUMMARY

- King Duncan asks his son, Malcolm, to confirm that the Thane of Cawdor has been executed.
- He is told that Cawdor died with dignity, repenting his actions.
- Macbeth and Banquo enter and are thanked by Duncan for their efforts in the war.
- Duncan proclaims that Malcolm will be his heir. He also says that he will visit Macbeth at home.
- Macbeth says he will write to his wife and prepare for the arrival of the king. He is unhappy about Duncan's announcement that Malcolm is next in line to the throne.
- In Macbeth's absence, Duncan praises him to Banquo.

CHECKPOINT 3   **A03**

How does the announcement of Malcolm as heir to the throne affect Macbeth?

WHY IS THIS SCENE IMPORTANT?

A   The King's announcement that Malcolm will be the next king provides Macbeth with **motivation** to prevent this happening by committing **murder** and **treason**.

B   Shakespeare shows how Macbeth's **attitude** has changed and hardened when he sees that Malcolm is in his way.

C   Macbeth's character is **contrasted** with those of Duncan, Banquo and even the executed Thane of Cawdor.

KEY LANGUAGE: CONTRAST   **A02**

Shakespeare reveals Macbeth's character through contrasts in this scene: between Duncan and Banquo, who are open and direct, and Macbeth, who hides his desires and intentions. Typically, for Duncan, 'stars, shall shine' (line 42), whereas for Macbeth they 'hide' so that darkness prevails (lines 50–1). We also hear of the former Thane of Cawdor's death, in which he showed repentance. This contrasts with the living Thane of Cawdor's evil ambition.

It is **ironic** that Duncan should comment about the former Thane of Cawdor that 'There's no art / To find the mind's construction in the face' (lines 11–12), since he so clearly fails to read what is in the new Thane of Cawdor's face. His trust of Macbeth leads to his death. Shakespeare's use of these contrasts serves to establish two contrary things: first, just how good and worthy a king Duncan is; second, just how appalling a crime it would be for Macbeth to murder him.

AIMING HIGH: CHARACTER DEVELOPMENT ⭐

In this scene Shakespeare shows that Macbeth's attitude to murdering the king has changed, even hardened. In Scene 3 the prospect, though desirable, was terrifying. His soliloquy (lines 49–54) reveals a new determination to carry it through. The vocabulary has switched from abstract, complex speech to simple matter-of-factness. **Couplets** reinforce the importance of the lines and the sense of inevitability about the deed Macbeth must do.

TOP TIP   A03

When writing about themes, try to link them to historical context. For example, if you are writing about gender, examine the roles of men and women in Shakespeare's time and compare those expectations then with those in today's society.

TOP TIP   A03

Notice how Lady Macbeth immediately understands what her husband's letter means. She taps into the supernatural world, inviting 'spirits' (line 25) to possess her.

ACT I SCENE 5: LADY MACBETH'S LETTER

SUMMARY

- Lady Macbeth reads a letter from her husband describing his encounter with the witches.
- She is convinced by the witches' prophecy because, as they promised, Macbeth has been made Thane of Cawdor.
- She worries that Macbeth is too kind-natured to be able to take the crown. She is determined that she will assist him through 'the valour of my tongue' (line 26).
- Lady Macbeth is overjoyed to learn that Duncan will stay in their castle overnight. She calls on demonic spirits to harden her resolve and to destroy any weakness or pity.
- Macbeth enters and she starts convincing him that he should murder Duncan.
- She insists that the deed must be done, that she will personally organise its operation, and finally that failure to accomplish it would be a form of fear.

WHY IS THIS SCENE IMPORTANT?

A   Shakespeare establishes the **close relationship** between Macbeth and his wife.

B   **Supernatural forces** are reintroduced with Lady Macbeth calling on them.

C   Her **language** heightens the scale of evil that she is contemplating.

D   We learn that Macbeth has 'human kindness' (line 16) in him that may conflict with his **ambition**.

KEY CHARACTERS: LADY MACBETH   A02

The letter to Lady Macbeth shows not only Macbeth's complete trust in his wife – for such a letter could be interpreted as treasonous – but also affection and love: 'my dearest partner of greatness' (line 10) suggests a warm equality. Later we will see how this affection cools.

KEY THEME: GENDER (A02)

There is a curious parallel between Lady Macbeth and the ambiguous sexuality of the witches. Lady Macbeth asks the spirits to 'unsex' her (line 40) and her 'woman's breasts' (line 46) are no longer to be used for milk but for murder. It is as if, at this level of evil, Lady Macbeth, like the witches, abandons being either male or female – becoming instead a neutral, 'it'. Later (I.7.46), Macbeth, in trying to deflect his wife's arguments, puts forward the view that in daring to do more than what is proper – or natural – for a man to do, one is no longer a man. Despite his argument, he does precisely that when he murders the king.

EXAM FOCUS: WRITING ABOUT MOTIFS (A02)

When writing about motifs, or recurring images, aim to look for different ways in which the image is used. Find examples from the whole text. Here is an example of writing about the motif of blood in *Macbeth*:

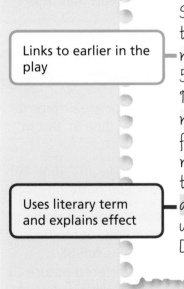

> Shakespeare uses the motif of blood throughout the play, starting with the bloody nature of battle in Act I Scene 2. In Act I Scene 5, Lady Macbeth demands that the spirits 'Make thick [her] blood'. Here blood is seen as a natural function of the human body, one that feeds the human capacity for compassion and repentance – things she does not want. 'Make thick my blood' is a metaphor, representing life and death. It is effective because it also makes us think of the blood she intends to shed – i.e. Duncan's.

Links to earlier in the play

Explains quotation

Uses literary term and explains effect

Now you try it:

Add two more paragraphs about the importance of blood in *Macbeth*. You could refer to the bloody daggers in Act II Scene 2 and the spot of blood that Lady Macbeth struggles to wash from her hands in Act V Scene 1.

KEY QUOTATION: KIND AND NURTURING (A02)

Lady Macbeth says her husband is 'too full o'the milk of human-kindness' (line 15). Shakespeare uses this metaphor to suggest that despite his reputation as a brave warrior, Macbeth also has a strong sense of compassion. Milk is mild, natural and, importantly, white. We associate this with purity, yet as the play progresses, Macbeth will be increasingly linked to the contrasting red of blood.

ACT I SCENE 6: DUNCAN ARRIVES AT MACBETH'S CASTLE

SUMMARY

- King Duncan arrives at Macbeth's castle, Glamis, with his sons, Banquo and attendant thanes.
- Lady Macbeth greets Duncan and they exchange compliments. Duncan takes her hand and is led into the castle.

WHY IS THIS SCENE IMPORTANT?

A Shakespeare continues developing the **theme** of **appearances** (loyalty to the king) versus reality (plotting to murder him).

B Shakespeare shows Lady Macbeth fully involved in the **deception** and the **treachery**.

C Duncan's open and generous nature is **contrasted** with that of the Macbeths.

KEY THEME: APPEARANCE AND REALITY (A02)

Once more Shakespeare shows how reality and appearance are different. The air appears 'delicate' (line 10) and the castle is 'loved' (line 5), but in reality this is to be the setting for foul murder.

Duncan asks after Macbeth with his new title, 'Thane of Cawdor?' (line 20) – ironically reminding us that the first Thane of Cawdor committed treason.

Lady Macbeth speaks of 'those honours deep and broad' (line 17) that Duncan has rewarded Macbeth with – while planning to murder him. Although she expresses appreciation for the honours, she is full of contempt, ingratitude and murder. She alludes to her two-faced nature when she says all her service is 'twice done and then done double' (line 15).

CHECKPOINT 4 (A01)

Shakespeare shows appearances can be deceptive: where else in the play is this evident?

TOP TIP (A03)

When writing about Duncan, you could think about whether he has any weaknesses as a character in spite of all his good qualities. Is it a weakness to be so trusting as a king?

TOP TIP: WRITING ABOUT KING DUNCAN (A01)

Duncan is a major character. His influence pervades the play and he sets the standard for what a king should be. Think about the following when writing about Duncan:

- When Shakespeare was writing, the king was considered to be next in line to God.
- Duncan is honest, sincere and above all, honourable. Macbeth describes Duncan as 'gracious' (III.1.65) after he has murdered him.
- The view of Duncan is consistent throughout the play (unlike views of Macbeth).
- He seems to enjoy the achievements of others and his gifts are not given to gain his own advantage.
- Our final view of Duncan is of him kissing his hostess Lady Macbeth. We later learn that he has sent her a diamond as a present (Act II Scene 1).

Consider how a contemporary audience would respond to such a king. How does his rule compare to Macbeth's?

ACT I SCENE 7: VAULTING AMBITION

SUMMARY

- In a soliloquy, Macbeth debates the pros and cons of murdering Duncan.
- He worries that the act of murdering his king and guest will return to plague him. He admits that Duncan has been a good king and worries that heaven itself will expose his wickedness.
- Macbeth says that the only justification for murder is his ambition.
- He is frightened by his own imagery of damnation and he resolves not to go ahead with the murder.
- Lady Macbeth enters and Macbeth informs her that he will not murder Duncan. He has been 'honoured' (line 32) recently by the king and does not want to 'cast aside' (line 35) this recognition.
- Lady Macbeth is contemptuous of his change of heart and accuses him of cowardice. They argue but her violent determination wins out. She outlines the plan and he agrees to it.

WHY IS THIS SCENE IMPORTANT?

A Shakespeare graphically shows Macbeth **wrestling** with his own **conscience** – the choice of evil is not inevitable or even easy for Macbeth.

B The major theme of **ambition** is stated overtly in this scene.

C Shakespeare shows Macbeth's **vulnerability** to accusations of cowardice and lack of manliness.

D Lady Macbeth's **responsibility** for what is to unfold is established.

E The idea that one murder will be sufficient – Macbeth's earlier hope – is already **undermined** in Lady Macbeth's immediate plan to implicate the guards.

KEY THEME: COURAGE AND MANLINESS (A02)

Lady Macbeth attacks her husband exactly where she knows it will hurt: his courage and manliness are at stake. And she does what she said she would do in Act I Scene 5, 'pour my spirits in thine ear' (I.5.25). Shakespeare demonstrates her strength of purpose and her leadership, which offer a remarkable contrast to Macbeth's performance at this stage.

Later, once he is king, Macbeth will appeal to Banquo's murderers in exactly the same way: if they are 'men' they will commit murder (III.1.91–107). At the end of the play, his courage and manhood are all that is left of him; so he fights Macduff knowing that he is doomed.

This is the critical scene in which all the arguments against treason and murder are explicitly and strongly made. Lady Macbeth demolishes each one, questioning her husband's manhood. Macbeth almost concedes that his wife is more manly than he is: her 'undaunted mettle should compose / Nothing but males' (lines 73–4). Thus, he falls into her way of thinking.

TOP TIP (A01)

Notice how Shakespeare uses his final words in this scene, 'False face must hide what the false heart doth know' (line 82), to echo Lady Macbeth's earlier advice about appearing as an 'innocent flower' whilst being 'the serpent under't'. (I.5.61–4).

ACT II SCENE 1: A DAGGER OF THE MIND

SUMMARY

● On his way to bed, Banquo has a premonition something is wrong, and then encounters Macbeth.

● Banquo presents him with a gift from the king: a diamond for Lady Macbeth.

● Banquo tells Macbeth that he dreamt of the witches. Macbeth says he does not think of them, but asks that he and Banquo speak about the matter another time.

● Macbeth is left alone and imagines he sees a dagger in front of him – a dagger that guides him towards his goal of killing Duncan.

● As the bell rings, he determines to go ahead and murder the king.

WHY IS THIS SCENE IMPORTANT?

A Shakespeare **intensifies** the **atmosphere** of darkness and evil.

B The **contrast** of Macbeth's thoughts with Banquo's integrity is made clear.

C Shakespeare shows us the **lasting effect** the witches have on Banquo – they disturb his dreams.

D Macbeth's **disloyalty** is highlighted by the king's gift, while his struggle with his **conscience** is decisively resolved.

> **CHECKPOINT 5** **A01**
>
> How does Shakespeare portray Banquo as appearing more open than Macbeth?

KEY CHARACTER: BANQUO

Shakepeare introduces Banquo at this point as another point of contrast with Macbeth. We see the witches have affected him – but whereas Macbeth has surrendered his will to them, only Banquo's dreams have been invaded.

Macbeth requests that they talk of the witches later with a promise to 'make honour for you' (line 26). This is an attempt to sound Banquo out – how will he react should Macbeth become king? Banquo's answer, which insists upon maintaining integrity, is hardly likely to please Macbeth. Shakespeare shows Banquo cannot be bought. It is not surprising that later Shakespeare has Macbeth comment that he feels 'rebuked' (III.1.55) by Banquo.

KEY SETTING: DARKNESS

Shakespeare depicts the scene as dark – torches are necessary to light the way. Banquo senses something is wrong. He notes that the stars' 'candles are all out' (line 5) – a metaphor suggesting that the physical darkness is also a moral darkness. He uses a simile to describe the effect on him: 'A heavy summons lies like lead upon me' (line 6). This adds to the weight of the atmosphere.

Later, when Macbeth is on his own, he sees a dagger in the dark. He is unsure whether this is real or a 'false creation / Proceeding from the heat-oppressèd brain' (lines 39–40)? The witches were real enough, but now Macbeth has embarked on evil he begins to see things that others cannot. Shakespeare shows that this image terrifies Macbeth, and this intensifies the atmosphere of evil.

ACT II SCENE 2: MACBETH MURDERS KING DUNCAN

SUMMARY

- Lady Macbeth's nerves are on edge as she waits for Macbeth to return from committing the murder. Her mood is bold, and she boasts about how she has drugged the guards.
- Macbeth enters, carrying two bloodstained daggers. He is obsessed by the noises of laughter and crying that he has heard.
- Macbeth's guilt torments him. Lady Macbeth attempts to lessen and rationalise his fears.
- She then criticises Macbeth for failing to leave the daggers on the guards. She has to go back herself and plant the weapons on them – Macbeth is too frightened.
- A knocking at the gate means they must quickly go to bed and pretend to be surprised when Duncan's body is discovered.

WHY IS THIS SCENE IMPORTANT?

A   Up until this point Macbeth had options – now there is **no going back**.

B   Shakespeare demonstrates the scale of the **terrifying guilt** that causes great warrior like Macbeth to be reduced to abject fear.

C   Lady Macbeth's character, by **contrast**, is shown by Shakespeare as steely and determined – where Macbeth flounders, Lady Macbeth perseveres.

KEY CHARACTER: LADY MACBETH (A02)

Despite some anxiety early on, Lady Macbeth is entirely in control of herself and of her husband. She planned the execution, and now it is her readiness of mind and strength of purpose that compensate for Macbeth's failure to act decisively once the murder is committed.

Shakespeare shows Lady Macbeth focused on the need to keep to the plan of action – ordering Macbeth to go back and place the daggers beside the guards, so as to incriminate them. Macbeth, however, is too terrified to return. He is much more concerned with the spiritual and moral implications of what he has done: the deep damnation, in fact, that he has brought upon himself.

KEY QUOTATION: OCEANS OF GUILT (A02)

In Macbeth's 'Will all great Neptune's ocean' (lines 57–60) speech, Shakespeare expands the language into the grandiose 'multitudinous seas incarnadine', and then just as suddenly deflates it into the simple 'green one, red'. Shakespeare uses sophisticated vocabulary to show that Macbeth is clouding his actions. The return to simple vocabulary brings Macbeth (and the audience) more immediately to the truth – he has killed the innocent King Duncan. Look for other places where the kind of language used gives us insights into a character or situation.

TOP TIP (A02)

Think creatively about Shakespeare's language. For example, the need for an 'Amen' (line 29), which Macbeth cannot speak, and the fact that even the ocean cannot clean him (lines 57–60), suggest that there is little hope for Macbeth.

ACT II SCENE 3: DUNCAN IS DISCOVERED

SUMMARY

- The knocking from the previous scene continues and the Porter goes to open the gate. He imagines he is the porter of Hell. He lets Macduff and Lennox in.
- Pretending to be awoken by the knocking, Macbeth arrives to greet them. Macduff asks to be led to the king.
- Macduff discovers the murder and returns, proclaiming treason. As Macduff calls the alarm, Macbeth and Lennox rush in to see Duncan.
- Lady Macbeth appears, then Banquo. Both are informed of the murder.
- Macbeth returns and bemoans the dreadful deed. Lennox suggests the guards may have been responsible and Macbeth confesses that he killed them.
- Macduff questions this action and Macbeth proclaims his love for Duncan. Lady Macbeth faints, distracting attention.
- Banquo says they must question the murder. Malcolm and Donalbain decide to flee, suspecting treachery from someone closely related.

WHY IS THIS SCENE IMPORTANT?

A   Shakespeare **anticipates** the horror of Macbeth's reign: the 'hell' the Porter mentions (lines 1, 17) later becomes a **reality**.

B   The **audience** already know that the murder has been committed so this delay in its discovery heightens the tension.

C   The themes of **murder** and **deception** are developed: the innocent guards are murdered to cover up the first crime.

D   Malcolm and Donalbain's escape will provide **justification** for Macbeth's coronation. However, it also means that he wears the crown uneasily, knowing they are alive and plotting against him. He will 'sleep no more' (II.2.40).

KEY STRUCTURE: COMIC RELIEF (A02)

The bleak intensity of the previous scene gives way to a brief comic interlude. The Porter is crude and rough and Shakespeare introduces him to make us laugh. However, his role also performs other key functions. The continued knocking reminds us that we are still in the world where the Macbeths commit murder.

KEY LANGUAGE: HELL (A02)

Much of the language in this scene is linked to ideas of hell, implying that the murder of the king has turned the castle into an underworld. The Porter refers to 'hell-gate' (line 2) and asks 'Who's there I'the name of / Belzebub?' (a name given to the devil) (lines 3–4). Lennox describes an 'unruly' (line 51) night in which the 'lamentings' and 'strange screams of death' (line 53) seem hellish.

Earlier references to a 'serpent' (I.5.65) and a 'chalice' (I.7.11) could suggest that the devil has entered into Macbeth. Later, Macduff will refer to Macbeth as a 'devil' (IV.3.56). Shakespeare seems to suggest there is a hell wherever Macbeth is.

CHECKPOINT 6 (A01)

Why does Macbeth kill the guards?

TOP TIP (A01)

Notice that the following themes are all present in this scene: deception, murder, distrust, fear and flight. Find evidence for each of them.

EXAM FOCUS: WRITING ABOUT HISTORICAL CONTEXT (A03)

In your essays it is essential to talk about the historical context linked to key moments in the play. Read this example of a student writing about historical context:

Shows specific knowledge of historical context

Some critics link the Porter's speeches to contemporary events: namely, the treasonous Gunpowder Plot of 1605. A Jesuit priest, Father Henry Garnet was hanged for lying about his knowledge of the Gunpowder conspiracy and pleaded that he did so for God's sake. Shakespeare uses this detail in the Porter's opening speech where he says 'here's an equivocator…who committed treason enough for God's sake'. A modern day audience might miss this allusion, but when the play was first performed the audience would understand the reference. The effect is to show that 'Hell' is not only on the stage in Macbeth's castle, but present in the society for which Shakespeare was writing.

Uses appropriate quotation to illustrate point

Describes effects on audience

Now you try it:

Expand on this paragraph by exploring other examples of traitorous behaviour in this play. You might refer to the Thane of Cawdor and the Macbeths' plot to kill their king.

ACT II SCENE 4: MACBETH BECOMES KING

SUMMARY

- Ross and an old man recall the dreadful night of the murder.
- Macduff enters and tells them that Duncan's two sons are suspected of paying the guards to commit the murder, because they have now fled.
- Macbeth has been nominated king and has gone to Scone to be crowned.
- Ross asks Macduff whether he will go to the crowning. Macduff says he will not, but will return home to Fife. Ross intends to go.

CHECKPOINT 7 **A01**

How key is the character of Macduff to the play?

WHY IS THIS SCENE IMPORTANT?

A Shakespeare uses this scene as a **buffer** between the high drama of the previous scene and the next when we meet the new king, Macbeth.

B The scene also acts as a **commentary** on all that has happened.

C The old man is important because he **represents the people**. In his memory these crimes are unparalleled.

D Shakespeare implies that Macduff is **suspicious** of Macbeth: he observes that the murderers were 'Those that Macbeth hath slain' (line 23) – and so could not be questioned – and that he will not go to Scone for the coronation.

KEY STRUCTURE: NARRATIVE PACE   **A02**

Act II is action-packed. In it we see the culmination of Macbeth's temptation. Where Act I is about Macbeth's desire for kingship, Act II delivers his treachery and murder: in Scene 1 we see Macbeth following the dagger; in Scene 2 we hear the two conspirators after the murder is done and witness Macbeth's fear and terror; in Scene 3 the Porter opens hell's gate and the murdered body is discovered, causing frantic commotion.

Now in Scene 4 Shakespeare allows us to pause, to reflect on the actions and events, yet at the same time provides further insights into the characters. Shakespeare subtly paints essential difference between Ross and Macduff – Macduff will avoid the coronation whereas Ross plans to attend. The old man, a minor character, provides an unbiased commentary on the unnatural events that have occurred. In this way Shakespeare prepares us for the next round of monstrous murders that Macbeth will initiate.

KEY QUOTATION: MOUSING OWL   **A01**

Shakespeare's use of **imagery** reminds us of how the natural order has been turned upside down. The old man emphasises how 'strange' (line 3) and 'unnatural' (line 10) the world has seemed since Duncan was murdered. He describes how a 'falcon towering in her pride of place/ Was by a mousing owl hawked at and killed.' (lines 12–13) There is a parallel between the falcon and King Duncan, whose life also comes to an unnatural end.

ACT III SCENE 1: MURDEROUS MACBETH

SUMMARY

- Banquo reflects on the witches' prophecies. He suspects that Macbeth obtained the crown through treachery.
- Macbeth and Lady Macbeth arrive.
- Macbeth pretends that he needs Banquo's advice on how to deal with Malcolm and Donalbain, who are abroad and spreading rumours.
- He learns details of Banquo's planned journey with his son, Fleance.
- Alone, Macbeth reveals that he fears Banquo. The thought of Banquo's offspring becoming kings is unacceptable to him.
- Two murderers are brought in. Macbeth outlines to them the reasons why Banquo is their mutual enemy. They agree to murder him and Fleance.

WHY IS THIS SCENE IMPORTANT?

- **A** Shakespeare shows us more about the **character** of **Banquo**. Unlike Macbeth, who is obsessed by the witches' prophecies, Banquo fears foul play.
- **B** Shakespeare reveals the **kind of rule** Macbeth offers: brutal and treacherous. Pretending to honour and value Banquo, his former comrade-in-arms, Macbeth casually works out his movements to entrap and murder him and his son.
- **C** We see Macbeth **persuading** others to commit crimes with the same key argument by which he himself was tempted: namely, to prove their manhood.
- **D** Lady Macbeth is **not** part of this plot.

KEY CHARACTER: MACBETH (A02)

Shakespeare demonstrates the depths to which Macbeth has sunk through his conversation with the murderers: here is a great warrior-hero who now has to meet the most vicious and corrupt kind of men in secret in order both to disguise and achieve his ends. The fact that he despises these men is shown in the way he addresses them. He interrupts the first murderer's solemn declaration of loyalty with the **ironic** 'Your spirits shine through you' (line 127). This suggests his contempt for the men.

In Act III Scene 3 we learn that Macbeth has employed a third murderer, showing how little he actually trusts the first two. But, then, trust is no longer something Macbeth believes in. Crucially, Lady Macbeth is no longer involved in his plans.

TOP TIP (A01)

Sometimes characters, like real people, are contradictory! Think about how on the one hand, Macbeth believes the prophecies must come true, and on the other, he seeks to prevent them happening. He commits murder so that he becomes king and then murders again to stop Banquo's offspring from attaining the crown.

CHECKPOINT 8 (A01)

Lady Macbeth is not involved in Macbeth's plan to kill Banquo. What does this suggest about Macbeth?

ACT III SCENE 2: SNAKES AND SCORPIONS

SUMMARY

- Lady Macbeth wants to speak to her husband before the feast. She is on edge – uncertainty and insecurity trouble them both.
- Macbeth appears and she scolds him both for staying alone and for his continued dwelling on their actions.
- They discuss the feast ahead, resolve to praise Banquo at it, and then Macbeth reveals his fear of Banquo and Fleance.
- He reveals that he intends to commit another dreadful crime. He will not tell Lady Macbeth what it is, but asks her to praise it when it is achieved.

WHY IS THIS SCENE IMPORTANT?

A   We see Macbeth growing in evil, and **hardening himself** to commit **more crimes**.

B   Duncan's peace of mind – being dead – is now a source of **envy** to Macbeth, who is in **torment** and has dreadful nightmares.

C   Lady Macbeth is no longer controlling and driving the action of her husband, but trying to **calm** his troubled mind.

D   The initial hope that they would enjoy their reign together is now exposed as **hollow**.

KEY CONTEXT **A03**

The Divine Right of Kings meant that because God appointed the king, he was not answerable to the people or to Parliament. Notice how differently Duncan and Macbeth are presented as rulers.

KEY CHARACTER: MACBETH **A02**

The third Act marks the turning point for our tragic hero. In the first part of the play we have seen Macbeth rise to power. Now he is king, he is hardening and becoming more brutal, and Shakespeare shows the situation changing. Macbeth keeps himself to himself and broods on the crimes committed, and on the crimes he intends to commit – notice the dark imagery: 'O, full of scorpions is my mind' (line 36). Just as scorpions bring death, so does the tormented Macbeth. He no longer shares his thoughts with his wife (in contrast to I.5.9–10) and so she feels isolated. The affectionate term, 'dearest chuck' (line 45) that Macbeth uses for her, seems to imply a shift in power.

For Lady Macbeth this scene marks the start of her breakdown – she will take control one more time, at the banquet (Act III Scene 4), after which she will be overwhelmed by remorse for the tide of evil she has helped unleash. Their roles are reversing.

ACT III SCENE 3: BANQUO IS MURDERED

SUMMARY

- The two murderers are joined by a third.
- They wait for Banquo and Fleance then spring out on them.
- They manage to kill Banquo, but in the confusion Fleance escapes.
- The murderers resolve to inform Macbeth of what has happened.

WHY IS THIS SCENE IMPORTANT?

A   Despite the precaution of adding a third murderer, Fleance **escapes** – the witches' **prophecy** is not easily avoided for all Macbeth's efforts.

B   The need to recruit a third murderer indicates Macbeth's **distrust** of the first two.

C   Where we did not see the actual murder of Duncan, but felt its horror, here Shakespeare makes us witness what is to become routine **assassination**.

KEY CHARACTER: MACBETH (A02)

The addition of a third murderer exposes the kind of world Macbeth now inhabits. He trusts no one, not even the accomplices he has commissioned. In the next scene (Act III Scene 4) we learn he has spies everywhere – everyone is being checked.

AIMING HIGH: LIGHT AND DARK ⭐

Notice how the theme of light and dark runs through the play, with Macbeth increasingly associated with darkness as his rule becomes more brutal. When the first murderer says 'The west yet glimmers with some streaks of day' (line 5) we can interpret the line as a metaphor showing that there is still some evidence of hope in the world. It also foreshadows the loss of life in the scene. When the third murderer asks 'Who did strike out the light?' (line

19) we can understand this to literally mean that the torch has been extinguished and also as a reference to the ending of Banquo's life.

In the previous scene, Macbeth noticed that 'Light thickens' (III.2.50). Arranging the murder of his friend is the final straw and brings an end to any chance of 'light' in Macbeth's future.

TOP TIP (A01)

The identity of the third murderer has caused much debate. Some have even suggested it is Macbeth in disguise! In the Polanski film version of the play Ross is depicted as the third murderer. Consider how key this character is to our further understanding of Macbeth.

ACT III SCENE 4: BANQUO'S GHOST

SUMMARY

- Macbeth welcomes various guests to his banquet.
- The first murderer appears and Macbeth steps aside to speak with him. The murderer tells Macbeth that Banquo is dead, but that Fleance escaped.
- Macbeth is disturbed. He returns to the feast and is gently reprimanded by his wife for his absence.
- He stands to raise a toast in praise of Banquo. As he does so, Banquo's ghost enters and sits in his place.
- Only Macbeth can see the ghost and Macbeth is terrified. Lady Macbeth says her husband often has these fits. Her quick thinking covers up for Macbeth as he begins to reveal his guilt.
- The ghost disappears and Macbeth regains his composure. Once more he tries to seem cheerful and praises 'our dear friend Banquo' (line 89). Then the ghost reappears and Macbeth loses his nerve altogether.
- He recovers when the ghost disappears again, but too late for the banquet to continue. Lady Macbeth dismisses everyone.
- Alone with his wife, Macbeth says that he thinks Macduff is against him. He reveals that he has spies in his lords' houses. He tells her that intends to revisit the witches.

> **CHECKPOINT 9** (A01)
>
> What do you think the thanes would be thinking after the banquet?

WHY IS THIS SCENE IMPORTANT?

A   Shakespeare shows the Macbeths at the **high point** of their careers – on their thrones, entertaining their subjects, all of whom (except Macduff) are prepared to accept them.

B   It ironically foreshadows the future: Banquo's ghost occupies Macbeth's seat, as his descendants will occupy his throne – and 'push us from our stools' (line 82).

C   It marks the beginning of the **decline** of Macbeth's rule and power: he cannot keep calm on this important occasion of state, and almost reveals his guilt.

D   The **supernatural** theme is evident.

E   It exploits **dramatic tension**. The audience see the murdered man appearing at a State banquet – will he be seen by others? Macbeth almost blurts out the truth of his **guilt** – will he be exposed?

F   We see that the **close bond** between Lady Macbeth and Macbeth is beginning to **dissolve**: she covers for him, but it is a strain on her. Macbeth no longer talks of 'we' but of himself.

KEY CHARACTERS: MACBETH AND LADY MACBETH (A02)

The strain on Lady Macbeth is evident. By the end of the scene, although he has been terrified, Macbeth seems casual in his attitude to what has happened. His comment, 'We are yet but young in deed' (line 144) suggests that this is a blip that will soon pass. Lady Macbeth, however, as Shakespeare shows, has had to use all her resources and wit to contain the potential damage of exposure.

Earlier she said 'Nought's had, all's spent' (III.2.4) and we see this particularly here: she wanted to be queen and the scene begins with her keeping 'her state' (line 5), in other words, remaining on her throne. If there was anywhere in the play where Lady Macbeth could enjoy being queen to the full, it is here: on her throne, surrounded by subjects. Yet, because of Macbeth's actions, this becomes a hollow and empty event, lacking any dignity or regal significance.

TOP TIP: WRITING ABOUT WITCHCRAFT AND PSYCHOLOGY (A02)

This scene raises the key question of witchcraft and psychology. Shakespeare develops the supernatural **motif** throughout the play: we have had the witches, their prophecies, the dagger that led Macbeth to Duncan, and now we have the ghost of Banquo. But whereas Banquo saw and heard the witches alongside Macbeth, here only Macbeth sees the vision. As Lady Macbeth says, 'When all's done, / You look but on a stool' (lines 67–8).

This has practical implications for any production of the play – is the ghost just in Macbeth's mind (and so is not shown on stage), or does a ghost really appear? Perhaps because of its sheer dramatic impact, most versions of the play tend to want to include it. When writing about the play it is important to decide whether you think Shakespeare intended us to believe in Banquo's ghost or to see it as a symptom of Macbeth's psychological distress.

TOP TIP (A02)

Consider that Shakespeare has structured the play so that this is the middle point: Act I is about plans against King Duncan, Act II show actions against King Duncan, Act III is the reign of Macbeth before Act IV, where plans against King Macbeth start, and finally, to complete the structure, Shakespeare shows the actions against King Macbeth in Act V.

KEY CONTEXT **A03**

The word 'weird' originally meant 'destiny' or 'fate'. The three Weird Sisters remind us of the three Fates of Greek mythology (Clotho, Lachesis and Atropos) who were thought to be more powerful than the gods and controlled the lives of mortals.

ACT III SCENE 5: THE WITCHES, HECAT AND MACBETH

SUMMARY

- The three witches and the goddess of witchcraft, Hecat, prepare a strong spell for deluding Macbeth.

WHY IS THIS SCENE IMPORTANT?

A   Shakespeare shows the **layers of evil**, revealing there are still depths that Macbeth can sink to.

B   Hecat refers to a 'dismal and a fatal end' (line 21) foreshadowing Macbeth's downfall.

C   Shakespeare links Macbeth to the **witches**, when Hecat refers to him as a 'wayward son' (line 11), implying that he has become fully evil in nature.

KEY THEME: EVIL   **A02**

Hecat suggests that Macbeth is a 'son' (line 11), although 'wayward', and this enables Shakespeare to indicate that Macbeth is no longer a victim of the witches' evil, but more a master – one of them – in their art. However, there can be no doubt – master or not – that by the end of the play he has so fully embraced evil, he has destroyed himself.

CHECKPOINT 10 **A01**

How is security Macbeth's 'chiefest enemy' (line 33)?

AIMING HIGH: LANGUAGE CHANGE

Understanding how language and meanings change over time is particularly useful when writing about Shakespeare. For example in this scene, Hecat refers to 'security' as an enemy of human beings (lines 32–3). This goes back to medieval Morality plays and is how Satan, the devil, tempts mankind by playing on their fears of future loss.

Nowadays, the word 'evil' tends to be reserved for extreme cases. People might refer to immoral actions as 'unacceptable' rather than evil. In the world of *Macbeth*, evil is an absolute that leads to a literal hell – as Macbeth himself is only too aware.

ACT III SCENE 6: LENNOX AND A LORD

SUMMARY

- Lennox outlines to another lord in deeply ironic terms his understanding of what has been happening in Scotland: that is, that Macbeth is responsible for all the murders that have plagued the state.
- Malcolm is in the English court attempting to raise military support to reclaim his throne. Lennox supports this.
- Macduff is in disgrace for refusing to attend Macbeth's banquet and is attempting to join Malcolm.

WHY IS THIS SCENE IMPORTANT?

A It shows the **direct consequence** of Macbeth's failure to control himself at his banquet: his lords have turned against him.

B It reveals that Macduff kept his **integrity** and went to Fife, not Macbeth's coronation.

C It outlines further the **deficiencies** in Macbeth's running of the state: not only the murders committed, but the lack of fairness and honour – in short, the corruption that blights everybody's life.

D We learn of hope in England, of Malcolm's welcome and of another kind of king – 'the most pious Edward' (line 27) – whom Shakespeare provides as another **contrast** with Macbeth.

KEY CHARACTER: MACDUFF

In Act III Scene 4, Macbeth says that he intends to 'send' (line 129) for Macduff. Act III Scene 6 confirms that he has sent for him and that Macduff has refused to attend. As Banquo is no longer a threat to Macbeth, Shakespeare provides another enemy, Macduff, who is beginning to challenge Macbeth's power.

It is Macduff who first questions Macbeth's behaviour after he kills the guards in Act II. Macduff asks 'Wherefore did you so?' (II.3.103), showing that he is suspicious of such rash behaviour. Shakespeare shows that Macbeth bitterly resents people, such as Banquo and Macduff, who have independent thoughts and ideas that might threaten his position of power, or reveal the truth about what he has done.

KEY QUOTATION: MACBETH IS UNPOPULAR A02

In this scene we learn that Macbeth's lords consider him to be a tyrant. A section of the lord's speech to Lennox reminds us of a prayer: 'Give to our tables meat, sleep to our nights.' (line 34) In his petitions for peace and food, the lord highlights the lack in their current lives. His request that they may 'Free from our feasts and banquets bloody knives' (line 35) shows the brutality of Macbeth's regime. The alliteration of 'banquets bloody' emphasises the lord's sense of anger at the tyranny.

KEY CONTEXT A03

The Lord's Prayer is a Christian prayer that is recorded in the New Testament of the Bible. In it there is an entreaty to God to 'Give us this day our daily bread'. The form of this prayer is echoed in this scene when the lord speaks to Lennox.

ACT IV SCENE 1: THE WITCHES' PROPHECIES

SUMMARY

- Three witches create a powerful spell and prepare to meet Macbeth. Hecat joins them and approves their spell.
- Macbeth then enters and commands them to answer his questions.
- They call up powerful spirits to respond to him.
- He is told three prophecies: that he should fear Macduff, that he cannot be harmed by one born of a woman and that he is secure until Birnan Wood comes to Dunsinane.
- He then presses them for more information about Banquo's offspring and is shown a vision of eight kings all descended from Banquo, who also appears.
- The witches suddenly vanish and Macbeth curses them. Lennox appears and informs Macbeth that Macduff has fled to England.
- Macbeth determines to kill Macduff's wife and children.

WHY IS THIS SCENE IMPORTANT?

A The spells show how **unnatural** the three witches are. Shakespeare offers a revolting level of detail with things like 'Eye of newt, and toe of frog' (line 14).

B Shakespeare portrays Macbeth's complete **confidence** in committing evil. He is implicit in the sorcery, and 'conjure[s]' (line 49) the witches.

C We learn that Macduff has **fled** to England in order to **challenge** Macbeth. Shakespeare creates dramatic tension by showing that Macduff escapes at the point when Macbeth is in pursuit.

D The irony of the prophecies **intensifies**: more are given, but they are double-edged. Shakespeare creates a sense of **anticipation** with this device.

TOP TIP (A03)

Look at a variety of images and film clips online to explore different ways in which this scene has been presented. Decide how you would like to see this staged.

KEY SETTING: THUNDER **A01**

Whenever the witches appear in *Macbeth* they are accompanied by thunder. This disturbance of nature reflects their evil intentions. Consider how you would stage the scenes with the witches. Shakespeare is not explicit about the location of this scene and various directors have set it in the outdoors and in caverns.

CHECKPOINT 11 **A01**

How does Shakespeare heighten the sense of evil in this scene?

KEY CHARACTER: MACBETH **A02**

In this scene we see Macbeth descending further into evil. Prior to his arrival, Macbeth is described by the witches as 'Something wicked' (line 45) – not even some*one*. Macbeth is one of their kind now, as they do a 'deed without a name' (line 49).

Shakespeare shows that earlier uncertainties have been stripped away. Before, the witches informed Macbeth of the prophecies; now he demands of them what he wants to know. He even threatens the powerful master spirits with a curse if they do not answer him (lines 104–5). When he leaves, there is no more agonising about what he needs to do – or discussing the situation with his wife – Macduff's castle is to be attacked. Notice the depths to which Macbeth has now fallen in deciding to murder women and children, without any pity.

EXAM FOCUS: WRITING ABOUT IRONY **A02**

In writing about *Macbeth* it is important to be able to comment on irony. Here is an example by one student of writing about irony in the play:

Clear explanation of irony in this scene

Irony is central to the play. Here, the irony is that all the prophecies are double-edged and turn against Macbeth. The witches say that 'none of woman born/Shall harm Macbeth' (lines 79–80), which builds Macbeth's confidence. However as we later learn, Macduff 'was from his mother's womb/Untimely ripped.' (V.6.54–5). Banquo's earlier comment accurately reflects the truth: 'The instruments of darkness tell us truths,/Win us with honest trifles, to betray's/In deepest consequence' (I.3.125–7). These words are prophetic and a condemnation of all that Macbeth comes to believe. Shakespeare has Banquo return once more in this scene (with his eight heirs) to mock the stability of Macbeth's throne.

Embedded quotation supports the point

Clear understanding of play as a whole

Now you try it:

Consider how irony affects the audience. Add another paragraph explaining how these examples might make us feel about Macbeth. For example, explore whether Shakespeare's use of irony makes us feel more or less sympathy for him.

ACT IV SCENE 2: MURDER OF MACDUFF'S SON

It is useful to look at different versions of *Macbeth* to understand how the scenes can be interpreted. For example, in Polanski's film version of *Macbeth*, Ross, after leaving Lady Macduff, actively assists in the murder by opening the door to let in the murderers. Think about how you would present the scene on stage.

SUMMARY

- Lady Macduff is with her son and Ross. Ross informs her that her husband has fled to England. Lady Macduff accuses her husband of cowardice. Ross makes his excuses and leaves.

- A messenger arrives, warns of danger, and leaves. Murderers enter, kill Macduff's son, and pursue Lady Macduff with the same purpose.

WHY IS THIS SCENE IMPORTANT?

A   Shakespeare shows the themes of **loyalty** and **treachery** being discussed and demonstrated.

B   We see the increasing **degradation** and **brutality** of Macbeth's reign: Banquo was assassinated for a purpose; Lady Macduff and her son, who are entirely innocent, are brutally murdered for pure spite.

C   Shakespeare uses the scene with all its **savagery** to evoke our **pity** and **sympathy** for the victims.

D   The character of Ross is that of the **diplomat** – always in the right place at the right time.

EXAM FOCUS: WRITING ABOUT STAGECRAFT   **A01**

In your essays it is important to remember that this is a play and intended for performance. Read this example of a student writing about stagecraft.

Uses evidence from the text

We do not see Lady Macduff murdered on stage (unlike her son), but we do hear her screaming 'Murder!' as she flees off stage. With this piece of staging, Shakespeare reinforces a central thematic idea. To have Lady Macduff murdered on stage would create a moment of fear and suspense, but the execution would be over immediately, and there would be another dead body left on the stage. Structurally, to see her fleeing off stage, screaming murder, prolongs the sense of suspense – we are not certain she is dead until the next scene. This is a natural consequence of the kind of fear that Macbeth detests – not knowing, not being sure. His reign has created this unease for everybody.

Explains the effect

Links to main character

Now you try it:

Add another paragraph in which you compare this scene with the ways in which Lady Macbeth and Macbeth himself die. Discuss the effects of staging for each.

ACT IV SCENE 3: MALCOLM AND MACDUFF

SUMMARY

- In England, Malcolm is suspicious of Macduff and tests him by pretending to be even more evil than Macbeth.
- Macduff's lament for Scotland convinces Malcolm who then retracts his confessions of evil. When he sees that that Macduff is sincere and opposed to Macbeth, Malcolm reveals that he has English support for an invasion of Scotland.
- Macduff is confused but pleased by this turn of events. A doctor appears and mentions the saintly work of King Edward the Confessor.
- Ross arrives and informs Macduff that his family has been murdered.
- Macduff resolves to support Malcolm and vows to kill Macbeth himself.

WHY IS THIS SCENE IMPORTANT?

A We see the **fear** and **suspicion** of Macbeth's reign in Scotland extend to England.

B Shakespeare provides a number of important **ideas** about what it means to be a **king**.

C Though this scene is '**static**' – a 'talking' scene – Shakespeare creates **dramatic tension**. He depicts Malcolm playing a game with Macduff and shows Ross's reluctance to reveal the truth about the massacre.

D Shakespeare sets up and **anticipates** the final **conflict** between Macbeth and Macduff.

E The scene provides a **balance** to the drama of Scenes 1 and 2 in Act IV: Macbeth's visit to the witches, and the murder of the Macduffs.

KEY CHARACTERS: MALCOLM AND MACDUFF (A02)

Malcolm is suspicious of Macduff because, as he says, 'He hath not touched you yet' (line 14), meaning that Macbeth has not injured Macduff (note Shakespeare's use of dramatic irony here, given the circumstances of the preceding scene). Malcolm has already experienced traitors who have tried to entrap him (lines 117–20), and is wary of committing himself.

KEY LANGUAGE: CONTRAST (A02)

Shakespeare often contrasts characters and their reactions to similar events. Macduff's reaction to the death of his wife might usefully be compared with Macbeth's reaction to news of Lady Macbeth's death (V.5.17–28). Shakespeare shows us how distraught Macduff is 'What, all my pretty chickens/and their dam, at one fell swoop?' (lines 217–18). Compare this with Macbeth's measured response 'Out, out, brief candle!' (V.5.23). The contrasting reactions emphasise how Macbeth has become desensitised to all normal human feeling.

CHECKPOINT 12 (A01)

Why does Malcolm pretend he is more evil than Macbeth?

TOP TIP (A01)

In trying to understand human character, it is useful to ask why Ross, in relating the death of Macduff's family, does not mention his own presence and conversation with Lady Macduff and his 'cousin' (IV.2.25) shortly before. What do you think is his reason?

ACT V SCENE 1: LADY MACBETH'S SLEEP WALKING

SUMMARY

- In Macbeth's castle at Dunsinane a doctor and a gentlewoman discuss their patient, Lady Macbeth.
- The gentlewoman refuses to discuss what she has heard Lady Macbeth say in her sleep, since she has no witness to back up her statements.
- As the doctor attempts to persuade her, Lady Macbeth appears, walking in her sleep.
- They both hear her reveal her guilt and watch her futile attempts to remove the blood from her hands.
- The doctor concludes that she is in need of spiritual rather than medical attention.

TOP TIP (A02)

Note the contrast between this scene and the previous: in Act IV Scene 3 we learn that the English king heals 'Evil' (IV.3.146), and here Lady Macbeth's disease is beyond the help of any doctor.

WHY IS THIS SCENE IMPORTANT?

- **A** It begins the **physical decline** of the Macbeths – Lady Macbeth is no longer in control.
- **B** Shakespeare reveals how **ordinary people** react to the enormity of the crimes committed by the Macbeths.
- **C** Shakespeare depicts the **psychological** 'truth' of a mental breakdown: the mental torture, the guilt and the obsession with the past.
- **D** Shakespeare portrays Lady Macbeth's condition as **sad**, but also the result of her own **choices**.
- **E** The **contrast** with Macbeth in Act V is marked: 'I cannot taint with fear' (V.3.3), he says. Until the prophecies start unravelling, Macbeth seems resistant to worry of any sort.

KEY FORM: PROSE AND BLANK VERSE (A02)

It is worth noting that Shakespeare wrote most of the play in blank verse. Notable exceptions are in the Porter's scene (Act II Scene 3) and this appearance of Lady Macbeth. Particularly in the first two Acts, Lady Macbeth's speech had been fiery blank verse – the strong rhythms reflecting her strong, determined grasp of reality. Now, she speaks in prose – choppy, abrupt, lurching from one incident to another, and even descending to doggerel with the rhyme of 'Fife' and 'wife' (line 38). Shakespeare's writing reflects what it means to 'break down'– even Lady Macbeth's language is breaking down under the strain. It is therefore not surprising that she commits suicide – she can no longer hold her life together, and with death, of course, language disappears altogether.

KEY QUOTATION: GUILT (A02)

After the murder of Duncan, Lady Macbeth says, 'What's done is done' (III.2.12), thus suggesting that the event should no longer be of concern. Here, Shakespeare shows that despite all her courage, ambition and strength of purpose, all that has been 'done' is not past, but present – and ever present – in Lady Macbeth's mind. She refers to her earlier words when she says, 'What's done cannot be undone' (lines 60–1) revealing her guilt.

KEY LANGUAGE: WATER AND WASHING (A02)

In this scene, Shakespeare reminds us of Lady Macbeth's earlier statement that 'A little water clears us of this deed' (II.2.65) with the physical symptoms of washing her hands. He also echoes Macbeth's insight after the murder when he asks 'Will all great Neptune's ocean wash this blood / Clean from my hand? No' (II.2.57–8). Although the Macbeth's share a common aim (to gain the throne), their beliefs are different. Ultimately, however, Shakespeare shows that neither a 'little water' nor an 'ocean' will wash away their guilt.

TOP TIP (A01)

Original and creative thinking about character is key for achieving higher grades. Consider the involvement of Lady Macbeth in the murder of Lady Macduff. Shakespeare does not explicitly link her to the decision to murder Lady Macduff, but she is clearly upset by the deed. Why do you think this is?

ACT V SCENE 2: THE REBELS

SUMMARY

- We are introduced to the rebel Scottish powers who are determined to join 'the English power' (line 1) at Birnan to overthrow Macbeth.
- The thanes comment on how Macbeth must feel uneasy now that his inadequacies and guilt are exposed. They are confident of victory.

WHY IS THIS SCENE IMPORTANT?

A   Shakespeare moves us from the **prospect** of action at the close of Act IV to the **actual** 'hurly-burly' of war – plans, preparations and advances.

B   Shakespeare uses this scene to add **tension** in the build-up to the **climax**.

C   We learn how **desperate** Macbeth's situation is: nobody supports him.

D   Shakespeare's mention of Birnan Wood and Dunsinane reminds us of the **prophecies**.

E   We see that the Scots, as well as the English are involved in **cleansing** Scotland.

KEY CONTEXT: PLAYING TO THE CROWN (A03)

Shakespeare ensures that the recovery of the crown by Malcolm is not solely through English forces; this is significant, particularly bearing in mind that the play was written while James (the First of England and Sixth of Scotland) was on the throne. In today's terms, Shakespeare was being 'politically correct' in his reference to contemporary events. King James was patron to Shakespeare's theatre company and we see Shakespeare taking this authority into account here.

TOP TIP (A01)

This scene builds tension and shows how unpopular Macbeth has become amongst his own men. How would you stage this?

KEY QUOTATION: IMAGERY OF CLOTHING (A02)

Notice how Shakespeare uses the imagery of clothing to show that Macbeth is simply not big enough to hold onto the crown. Angus says Macbeth 'does feel his title/Hang loose about him like a giant's robe/Upon a dwarfish thief' (lines 20–2). In this almost comical simile the comparison between Macbeth and a thief emphasises the men's disrespect for their leader.

ACT V SCENE 3: FEARLESS MACBETH

SUMMARY

- Macbeth enters with the doctor and attendants.
- He is in a fearless mood: the prophecies give him complete confidence that he is untouchable.
- A servant is jeered as he reports that the English troops are arriving.
- Macbeth orders his armour and asks the doctor to cure his wife.
- He dismisses the doctor's medical advice and asks him instead what would cure his country.
- He scarcely listens to the doctor's reply – he is obsessed with the prophecies, which he thinks are the only things that will guarantee his security.

TOP TIP **A02**

Notice how Macbeth dominates this scene. He speaks using imperatives – giving commands to all those around him. Make a list of all the demands he makes from the start to the end of the scene.

WHY IS THIS SCENE IMPORTANT?

A Shakespeare shows Macbeth as **fearless**, but also **desperate** – he has come to totally depend on the **prophecies** as his sole source of information and support.

B We see how Macbeth's **reign of terror** extends to all those around him. His contempt for his servant and the doctor explain how his brutality has led to a lack of support.

C Shakespeare's use of the doctor character suggests that Scotland itself needs **healing**.

EXAM FOCUS: WRITING ABOUT HEALTH **A02**

The theme of health is important in this scene. Here is one student's writing about this subject:

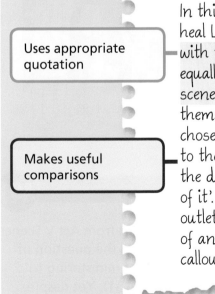

Uses appropriate quotation

In this scene we hear how the doctor cannot heal Lady Macbeth. He says that she is 'troubled with thick-coming fancies' (line 38). This applies equally to Macbeth, who starts and ends the scene by talking about the prophecies which in themselves can be seen as 'fancies'. He has chosen to believe them and live his life according to them. Like his wife, he is obsessed. He rejects the doctor's advice about healing, with 'I'll none of it'. Instead his restless energy seeks violent outlets - the casual way he orders the hanging of anyone talking of fear (line 36) shows how callous and depraved he has become.

Refers to the scene as a whole

Makes useful comparisons

Now you try it:

Examine another part of the play where healing is referred to and compare with this one. You might look at Act IV Scene 3 where the Doctor explains how the King of England seems to have a miraculous healing touch.

ACT V SCENE 4: GREAT BIRNAN WOOD RISES

SUMMARY

- Malcolm orders his men to each cut down a bough from Birnan Wood and to carry it in front of them to conceal their numbers from Macbeth.
- They learn that Macbeth intends to remain in Dunsinane, his strategy being to endure a siege.
- This is his only hope, since his troops are demoralised and fight for him out of necessity, not commitment.

WHY IS THIS SCENE IMPORTANT?

A Shakespeare creates **tension** by showing us the preparations going on in the camp opposing Macbeth.

B We are reminded of the **prophecy** that Macbeth will be safe until Birnan Wood rises up and moves to Dunsinane.

C The **influence** of the **witches**, and of the **supernatural** is felt in this scene.

TOP TIP (A01)

Have a look at *Tales from Shakespeare* by Marion Williams (1998) that includes *Macbeth*. This is a modern retelling with excellent illustrations and some quotations from the play.

KEY STRUCTURE: TRAGEDY

In the previous scene, Shakespeare reintroduces the doctor from Act V Scene 1, providing a neat sense of continuity and dramatic irony: the question of ministering to Lady Macbeth extends to the wider issue of ministering to the country, which has, as Macbeth notes, a 'disease' (line 51). Yet despite that, there is a part of him which still evokes compassion: his recognition of the life he might have had – which included 'honour', 'love' and 'troops of friends' (lines 24–5) – cannot but touch the heart. He knows, and relishes, what is good – but has chosen the opposite. This is his tragedy.

That Macbeth is doomed should be obvious from the previous scene: the dependence he now has on the prophecies is paralysing his own decision-making and capacity for action. 'Bring me no more reports' (line 1) is a desperate statement for someone engaged in a war to utter – intelligence-gathering is of primary importance. In contrast in Act V Scene 4, we see the practical preparations for an attack on Macbeth's castle. The audience realise that Macbeth's obsession with the prophecies will lead to his downfall, as we see Malcolm's soldiers preparing to 'move' Birnan Wood to Dunsinane.

CHECKPOINT 13 (A01)

How do the prophecies destroy Macbeth?

AIMING HIGH: WRITING ABOUT SHAKESPEARE'S STAGECRAFT ⭐

You should aim to write about how Shakespeare structures the play to create impact and increase tension.

Notice how Shakespeare uses structure in Act V to simply and effectively increase tension. Scene 1 led us into the diseased mind of Lady Macbeth; in Scene 2 we switched to the preparation of the Scottish thanes who were planning to attack Macbeth. Scene 3 returned us to the castle – we witnessed Macbeth's diseased mind, but were also made much more aware of Scotland's disease.

Now, in Scene 4, we return to the cure for all these diseases: the English army led by Malcolm, the rightful king. As Seyward concludes: 'certain issue strokes must arbitrate' (line 20) – a bloody operation is required to remove the 'disease' of Macbeth's rule. We have seen the situation in both camps. Now the battle must commence.

ACT V SCENE 5: THE QUEEN IS DEAD

SUMMARY

- Macbeth enters boasting that he is confident of victory.
- A woman's scream is heard and Seyton goes to investigate. Macbeth reflects that nothing terrifies him now.
- Seyton returns with news that the queen is dead. This is confirmation for Macbeth that life is meaningless.
- A messenger arrives to tell him that Birnan Wood is moving towards Dunsinane Castle.
- Outraged, and in doubt about his destiny, Macbeth orders an attack.

WHY IS THIS SCENE IMPORTANT?

A   Lady Macbeth dies – the final end of her **ambitions.** Shakespeare shows us Macbeth reflecting on the **meaninglessness** of life.

B   The **prophecies** start **unravelling**, and Macbeth, who has so blindly followed them, is derailed from his strategy to hold the castle. Shakespeare shows us how accepting the prophecy leads directly to Macbeth's **downfall.**

C   Macbeth's key characteristic is again **courage**, as he goes out to face his enemies and fight them.

TOP TIP   (A01)

Examine contrasts in the play. For example, contrast the deaths of Lady Macduff and Lady Macbeth, and explore the reactions of their husbands, to make clear you understand the differences in their characters. Compare Macbeth's mood in this scene with that of the attackers. Notice how his confidence contrasts with their humility.

AIMING HIGH: LADY MACBETH'S DEATH

Shakespeare portrays Lady Macbeth's death as inevitable. It is effective (and symmetrical when we consider Lady Macduff's end) to hear her final scream rather than witness her death. It seems that she has committed suicide. Macbeth's reaction to it can be read in a number of ways. When writing about the death of the queen, consider the following:

- Is Macbeth entirely indifferent and emotionless – 'Signifying nothing' (line 28)?
- Does his soliloquy suggest cynicism as a last response – 'Told by an idiot' (line 27)?
- Or does the word 'hereafter' (line 17) signify his acknowledgement of the real loss in his life?

Shakespeare presents Macbeth's isolation – he is suffering and despite our revulsion for all that he stands for, we cannot help but pity him here. Notice Macbeth's state of mind: 'I 'gin to be aweary of the sun' (line 49) – he no longer cares whether he lives or dies.

ACT V SCENE 6: THE FINAL DOWNFALL OF MACBETH

SUMMARY

- Malcolm, Macduff and Seyward, with their armies camouflaged, approach Macbeth's castle. Battle commences.
- Macbeth kills Young Seyward in combat. He is trapped but unbeaten, even though his army has fallen.
- Macbeth encounters Macduff, who reveals that he was not 'born' of woman (line 13), but delivered by Caesarean (lines 15–16). In a final act of courage Macbeth fights Macduff and is killed.
- While Malcolm comforts Seyward over the death of his son, Macduff arrives with Macbeth's head and hails Malcolm King of Scotland.

WHY IS THIS SCENE IMPORTANT?

- **A** Shakespeare shows the full extent of Macbeth's **belief** in the witches.
- **B** Our curiosity about the **prophecies** – especially about someone not born of a woman – is satisfied.
- **C** Despite all the witches have done to enslave Macbeth, Shakespeare demonstrates that his **courage** remains intact.
- **D** The **waste** and **futility** of Macbeth's reign is summarised in the death of Young Seyward.

KEY CHARACTER: MACBETH'S COURAGE (A02)

Shakespeare presents Macbeth primarily as a warrior, and this is significant in our final evaluation of him. By giving in to the temptation that the witches offer, he loses almost every aspect of his true humanity. Even his courage temporarily deserts him (V.8.18) when he learns from Macduff how false the prophecies are – yet his courage returns at the end: he will not yield. He will take on Fate as well as Macduff – 'Yet I will try the last' (V.8.32) – and this, while it does not excuse his crimes, does enable us to see some remnant of his great bravery.

Shakespeare establishes Macbeth's ferocious qualities as a fighter early on and we are reminded of his true strength in this final scene. This is important as without it, Macduff's achievement in slaying him in one-to-one combat is diminished.

> **KEY CONTEXT (A03)**
>
> The themes of revenge and retribution feature strongly in Greek Tragedy, showing the influence of classical forms on Shakespeare's writing.

KEY THEME: BETRAYAL (A01)

The theme of betrayal comes full circle. Just as Macbeth betrayed Duncan, so the witches have betrayed Macbeth. In Act I, when deliberating the pros and cons of treason and murder, Macbeth says 'we but teach/Bloody instructions, which, being taught, return/To plague the inventor' (I.7.8–10). Shakespeare shows this, too, has come true. Macbeth has had no rest as his own men and thanes have constantly defected from his cause, and his ultimate trust in the witches also proves misplaced. They are 'juggling fiends' (V.8.19). Banquo warned him about them in Act I and now Macbeth has experienced what Banquo predicted.

PROGRESS AND REVISION CHECK

SECTION ONE: CHECK YOUR KNOWLEDGE

Answer these quick questions to test your basic knowledge of the play, its characters and events:

1. Who is with Macbeth when he first meets the witches in Act I?

2. What do the witches predict will happen to Macbeth?

3. Who tells Macbeth that he is Thane of Cawdor?

4. How does Macbeth communicate the news of the witches' prophecy to his wife?

5. What does Lady Macbeth call on to give her strength?

6. How does she persuade Macbeth to go through with the murder?

7. Who do the Macbeths plan to blame for killing Duncan?

8. What else does Macbeth murder?

9. Where do Malcolm and Donalbain go?

10. Whose mind is 'full of scorpions' (III.2.36)?

11. How many murderers does Macbeth employ to kill Banquo and his son?

12. Whose ghost appears at the feast?

13. What ingredients do the witches add to their cauldron?

14. Who should Macbeth beware of?

15. How many kings do the witches show to Macbeth?

16. Who are the 'pretty chickens' (IV.3.217)?

17. Where does Lady Macbeth appear to see a 'damned spot' (V.1.33)?

18. How does Birnan Wood move to Dunsinane?

19. Who tells Macbeth his wife is dead?

20. How does Macbeth die?

SECTION TWO: CHECK YOUR UNDERSTANDING

Here are two tasks about the significance of particular moments in the play. These require more thought and slightly longer responses. In each case, try to write at least three to four paragraphs.

Task 1: Act I Scene 1: How does this opening scene with the witches establish the mood and key themes for the rest of the play?

Think about:

- Language – in particular the apparently contradictory 'Fair is foul, and foul is fair.' (I.1.9)
- Stagecraft – how atmosphere could be created on stage with this scene.

Task 2: Act III Scene 2: How does Shakespeare show the change in the Macbeths' relationship in this scene? Compare their relationship here with Act I Scene 7.

Think about:

- Language – compare Lady Macbeth's persuasive language in Act I Scene 7 with her more submissive language here.
- Themes – notice how the theme of ambition is presented in each scene.

PROGRESS CHECK

GOOD PROGRESS

I can:

- understand how Shakespeare sequences and reveals events. ☐
- refer to the importance of key events in the play. ☐
- select well-chosen evidence, including key quotations, to support my ideas. ☐

EXCELLENT PROGRESS

I can:

- refer in depth to main and minor events and how they contribute to the development of the plot. ☐
- understand how Shakespeare has carefully ordered or revealed events for particular effects. ☐
- draw on a range of carefully-selected key evidence, including quotations, to support my ideas. ☐

WHO'S WHO?

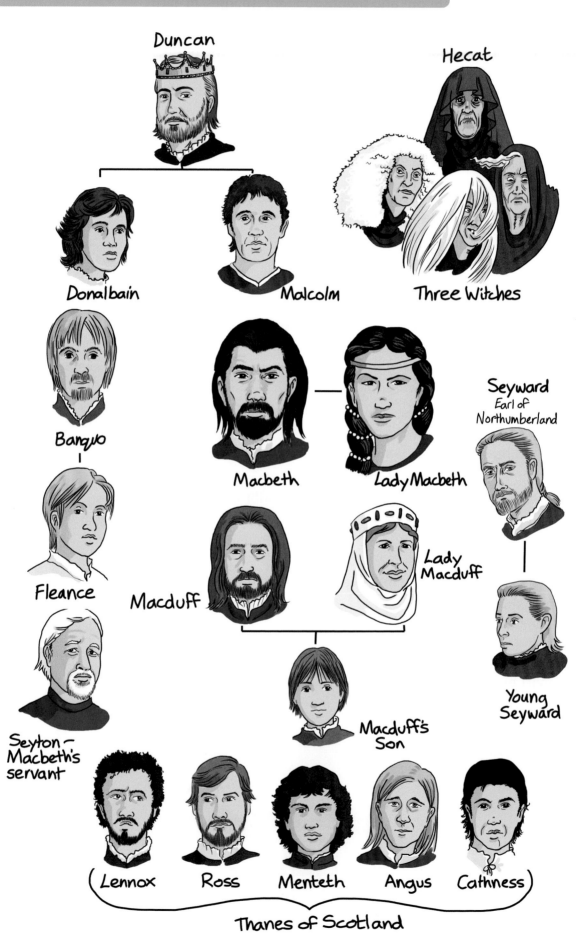

Duncan

Hecat

Donalbain

Malcolm

Three Witches

Banquo

Macbeth

Lady Macbeth

Seyward
Earl of
Northumberland

Fleance

Macduff

Lady
Macduff

Seyton –
Macbeth's
servant

Macduff's
Son

Young
Seyward

Lennox   Ross   Menteth   Angus   Cathness

Thanes of Scotland

KING DUNCAN

DUNCAN'S ROLE IN THE PLAY

Duncan is the King of Scotland. He is well liked and respected by his people. He is known for being a just and honest ruler. Macbeth and his wife murder him in his sleep so that Macbeth can take the crown. In the play, Duncan:

- listens to reports of Macbeth's actions in battle and praises his courage (I.2).
- decrees that Macbeth will have the title when he learns that the Thane of Cawdor has been treacherous (I.2).
- praises Banquo for his worthiness and makes Malcolm heir to his throne (I.4).
- visits the Macbeths at Dunsinane and greets Lady Macbeth warmly (I.6).
- sends Banquo with a diamond as a gift for Lady Macbeth (II.1).
- is murdered by Macbeth (II.2).

EXAM FOCUS: WRITING ABOUT DUNCAN

Key point	Evidence/Further meaning
• He is generous, bestowing honours on his warriors and gifts on their wives.	• 'More is thy due than more than all can pay' (I.4.22). • He says he cannot praise Macbeth enough.
• He is fair and just in his leadership.	• 'this Duncan/Hath borne his faculties so meek, hath been/So clear in his great office' (I.7.16–18).
• Duncan is well-respected and liked.	• 'tears shall drown the wind' (I.7.25). • When Macbeth contemplates his motives for murder he thinks about how Duncan's death will be mourned.

TOP TIP: WRITING ABOUT LEADERSHIP

Notice how Duncan's leadership contrasts entirely with Macbeth's. Where Duncan is trusting and generous, Macbeth is suspicious and tyrannous. Duncan is presented as a fair and gentle king. It's important you can discuss how this affects the audience's response to his murder.

MACBETH

MACBETH'S ROLE IN THE PLAY

Macbeth is a warrior and the Thane of Glamis. His ambitions lead him to betray and murder his king to take the throne of Scotland. In the play, Macbeth:

- defeats the armies of the rebellion against King Duncan (I.2).
- meets three witches who prophesy that he will be king.
- plots with his wife to murder Duncan and assume the throne (I.7, II.2, 4).
- arranges for his friend, Banquo, to be murdered (III.2, 3) in fear of the witches' prediction that Banquo's children will be kings.
- has Macduff's family killed on the basis of further prophecies.
- is cornered by English and Scottish forces, and killed in single combat by Macduff.

TOP TIP   (A02)

Consider the extent to which the witches are to blame for the death of Duncan. Is Macbeth's ambition or their prophecy the real reason for his actions?

MACBETH'S IMPORTANCE TO THE PLAY AS A WHOLE

Macbeth is the fatal protagonist of the play whose tragic rise and fall is told. Although he is initially presented as brave and valiant, we witness how ambition drives Macbeth to betrayal, brutality and ultimately his death.

EXAM FOCUS: WRITING ABOUT MACBETH   (A01)

Key point	Evidence/Further meaning
• Macbeth is first and foremost a warrior – courage is his defining quality.	• 'For brave Macbeth – well he deserves that name' (I.2.16). • The Captain describes Macbeth's bravery in battle.
• He is not essentially a brutal character. In fact, Lady Macbeth worries that her husband might be too kind to kill the king.	• 'Yet do I fear thy nature; / It is too full o'the milk of human-kindness / To catch the nearest way' (I.5.14–16). • Mildness and pure white colour of milk suggests Macbeth has these attributes too.
• Banquo observes that the witches' prophecies have come true, but he fears his friend has accelerated events with dishonesty.	• 'Thou hast it now: king, Cawdor, Glamis, all, / As the weird women promised, and, I fear, / Thou play'dst most foully for't' (III.1.1–3). • Echoes the witches claim that 'fair is foul' (I.1.9).
• Finally, Macbeth is thought of as a mass murderer.	• 'this dead butcher' (V.6.108). • Malcolm does not even use his name.

TOP TIP: WRITING ABOUT TRAGEDY (A01)

When you are writing about Macbeth always remember that the play is the 'tragedy' of Macbeth. In other words, Shakespeare does not present him as a wholly bad person. At the start of the play he has good qualities. He changes under the influence of the witches and his wife. You need to balance his final condition – the treacherous, mass murderer under the sway of supernatural forces – with his earlier and finer qualities: his love of his wife, his sensitive imagination and bravery. Ask, what remains at the end? Ensure your answer is balanced.

KEY QUOTATION: A FATAL FLAW (A02)

At the end of his soliloquy, Macbeth admits he has 'no spur/To prick the sides of my intent, but only/Vaulting ambition' (lines 25–7). This reveals his fatal flaw to the audience, and suggests the tragedy to come. Shakespeare shows us that Macbeth knows King Duncan is 'meek' and 'great' (lines 17–18) but still his ambition is stronger than his respect.

TOP TIP (A03)

Don't forget, Shakespeare places Macbeth between two opposing forces: the witches who are evil and God who is good. Macbeth is human, and so a mixture of good and evil. This is what interests us about him.

KEY THEME: SECURITY (A01)

Macbeth has been obsessed with the need for security since assassinating Duncan. Shakespeare portrays him as frightened of what he cannot control. This is shown in his need to visit the witches and find the certainty of 'security' (III.5.32). One factor in establishing the trustworthiness of the prophecies in Macbeth's mind is the speed with which they happen: he becomes 'Cawdor' (I.3.106) immediately after the witches say he will; now, having been told to watch out for Macduff, Shakespeare has Lennox appear with the same warning. The effect of this is that Macbeth (and, to an extent, the audience) feels secure at this point that the prophecies can be trusted.

REVISION FOCUS: MACBETH'S TRANSFORMATION

Consider how Macbeth changes throughout the play. Make a chart to show how he descends into a moral abyss. Choose a series of key moments and quotations to record his fall and add these to your graph. Learn the pattern of these events so that you can write confidently about his character development.

TOP TIP: MAKING CONNECTIONS (A02)

Look for original and powerful connections between characters. For example, Banquo and Macduff are linked by their opposition to Macbeth; Lady Macbeth and Lady Macduff both die, though in very different circumstances. You could focus on how Macbeth is tempted. Contrast this with how Banquo is tempted, but does not give way.

LADY MACBETH

LADY MACBETH'S ROLE IN THE PLAY

Lady Macbeth is the ambitious wife of Macbeth, who encourages him to murder his king, helps him to do it, and so becomes queen of Scotland. In the play, Lady Macbeth:

- invokes the powers of evil to help her influence her husband (I.5, I.7) to commit murder and treason.
- subsequently acts the perfect hostess to the king in a false display of duty and affection (I.6).
- is an accomplice in the murder and in establishing an alibi in the form of Duncan's guards (II.2, 3).
- uses quick thinking and presence of mind to save Macbeth from admitting his guilt to the thanes when Banquo's ghost appears at their banquet (III.4).
- is increasingly isolated from her husband and begins to sleep walk.(V.1).
- is obsessed with nightmares of her actions and finally commits suicide (V.5).

TOP TIP (A01)

Lady Macbeth is dominant, cunning, determined and haunted. These four aspects could make up the core elements of an essay response on her character.

LADY MACBETH'S IMPORTANCE TO THE PLAY AS A WHOLE

As Macbeth's wife, she persuades her husband to commit murder and helps him to cover up his actions. Her downfall precedes Macbeth's, as guilt and isolation lead to her mental breakdown and death.

EXAM FOCUS: WRITING ABOUT LADY MACBETH (A01)

Key point	Evidence/Further meaning
● Duncan trusts Lady Macbeth as the gracious wife of one of his most important lords.	● 'our honoured hostess' and 'Fair and noble hostess' (I.6). ● The repetition of 'hostess' emphasises how inhospitable her actions will be.
● Macbeth has affection for his wife, and trusts her to help him with his plans.	● 'my dearest partner of greatness' (I.5.9). ● He sees her as an equal.
● Macbeth compliments his wife by saying her strength makes her like a man.	● 'Bring forth men-children only!/For thy undaunted mettle should compose/Nothing but males' (I.7.72–4). ● There is nothing 'soft' or feminine in her.
● Malcolm's final judgement is that Lady Macbeth was like a devil.	● 'fiend-like queen' (V.6.108). This associates her with hell.

AIMING HIGH: AGENT OF THE SUPERNATURAL? ⭐

Shakespeare does not present Lady Macbeth as equal to Macbeth – it is not *their* tragedy, but his. Her role, however, is vital: Macbeth is tempted to do evil and Lady Macbeth is the key human agent – the one Macbeth trusts and loves – who ensures his temptation is thorough and complete. Some interpretations of the play connect her to the witches: it is Lady Macbeth who seems determined to bring about their prophecy. The way she calls on the spirits of evil seems to parallel the witches' spells. Despite her initial overpowering presence, she is not a heroic character herself. This is shown in her collapse once Macbeth withdraws his confidence from her.

TOP TIP: WRITING ABOUT LADY MACBETH (A02)

Lady Macbeth immediately understands what her husband's letter means. Her response is direct and to the point: her husband must be what he has been promised – King of Scotland. No fine points of conscience or loyalty seem to worry her, and it is noticeable how Shakespeare portrays her as overwhelming her husband when he appears. It is also interesting to reflect on how she taps into the supernatural world: her 'spirits' (line 25) will invade Macbeth's ear in the form of her manipulative language; and she literally invites spirits to possess her body.

AIMING HIGH: APPEARANCE AND REALITY ⭐

The play raises questions about appearance and reality. Does the supernatural really exist and have such powers? Did Shakespeare believe in a supernatural realm? Is the appearance of the supernatural in *Macbeth* a metaphor for mental disturbances in the characters, such as the sleepwalking of Lady Macbeth? In Shakespeare's time people generally believed in witchcraft. The King, James I deemed it a capital offence to be a witch, considering them enemies to society. We could argue that within the play the witches are real, and an attempt to present the play purely in psychological terms does not match Shakespeare's conception. But can we say the same for Macbeth's visions? As he waits to kill Duncan, Macbeth sees a dagger in front of him. 'Is this a dagger which I see before me' (II.1.33). This could be a ghostly apparition, drawing him to action, or it could be understood as a disturbance of the mind. What difference does each interpretation make to our understanding of *Macbeth*?

KEY CONTEXT (A03)

It is a useful to consider the historical role of women when writing about Lady Macbeth. To what extent does she conform to the contemporary ideal of womanhood?

KEY QUOTATION: LADY MACBETH'S USE OF PROSE (A01)

Lady Macbeth usually speaks in blank verse. After reading the letter from her husband, which is written in prose, she calls on demons and plans murder. Later, when she is sleepwalking, she speaks in prose: 'Out, damned spot! Out, I say! – One: two: why/then, 'tis time to do't' (V.1.33–4). The lack of blank verse here reflects her mental disorientation.

BANQUO

BANQUO'S ROLE IN THE PLAY

Banquo is Macbeth's honourable and loyal friend. He resists the temptation presented by the witches and is later murdered by Macbeth. In the play, Banquo:

- helps defeat the enemies of King Duncan in battle (I.2).
- receives prophecies from the witches along with Macbeth (I.3).
- warns Macbeth against trusting the prophecies (I.3).
- suspects something before and after the murder (II.1, II.3, III.1).
- is assassinated at Macbeth's orders while out riding with his son (III.3).
- appears as a ghost to Macbeth and disrupts his celebrations (III.4).
- appears as an apparition in the witches' cave, confirming that his offspring will become future kings of Scotland and more (IV.1).

EXAM FOCUS: WRITING ABOUT BANQUO (A01)

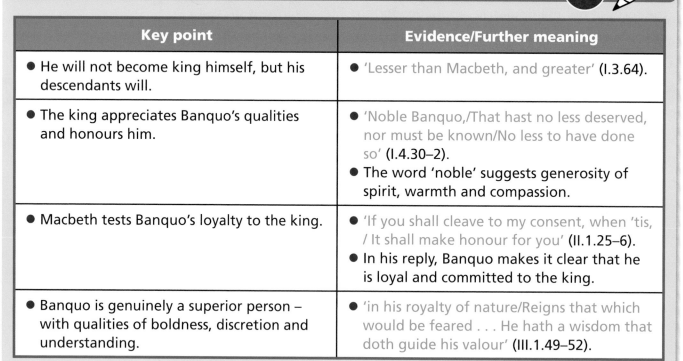

Key point	Evidence/Further meaning
• He will not become king himself, but his descendants will.	• 'Lesser than Macbeth, and greater' (I.3.64).
• The king appreciates Banquo's qualities and honours him.	• 'Noble Banquo,/That hast no less deserved, nor must be known/No less to have done so' (I.4.30–2). • The word 'noble' suggests generosity of spirit, warmth and compassion.
• Macbeth tests Banquo's loyalty to the king.	• 'If you shall cleave to my consent, when 'tis, / It shall make honour for you' (II.1.25–6). • In his reply, Banquo makes it clear that he is loyal and committed to the king.
• Banquo is genuinely a superior person – with qualities of boldness, discretion and understanding.	• 'in his royalty of nature/Reigns that which would be feared . . . He hath a wisdom that doth guide his valour' (III.1.49–52).

TOP TIP: WRITING ABOUT BANQUO (A01)

If Macbeth succumbs to evil forces and suggestions, then Banquo is his opposite. Shakespeare presents both men as warriors and thanes; both see and hear the witches, but at every point Banquo seems to stand up for honour and integrity. However, one weakness proves to be his undoing: his unwillingness to reveal what he knows. He suspects that Macbeth has 'playedst most foully' (III.I.3) to make the witches' prophecies happen, but he tells no one. This omission costs him his life: he fails to realise he will be Macbeth's next victim.

MACDUFF

MACDUFF'S ROLE IN THE PLAY

Macduff is the honourable thane who ultimately brings retribution to Macbeth. He is the man of destiny, 'not born of woman' (V.3.6). In the play, Macduff:

- discovers Duncan's murder (II.3).
- suspects Macbeth's guilt and refuses to attend his coronation (II.4). Macbeth begins to fear him (III.4).
- abandons his castle and flees to England without his family (IV.1). His family are murdered in his absence (IV.2).
- hunts out and kills Macbeth in single combat (V.8).

EXAM FOCUS: WRITING ABOUT MACDUFF

Key point	Evidence/Further meaning
• Macduff's peers hold him in esteem and affection.	• Referred to by Banquo as, 'Dear Duff' (II.3.86).
• Macbeth goes from hot to cold in his reaction to Macduff; at his deepest level he knows he should fear Macduff – a warrior too – which is why he attempts to destroy him.	• 'Then live, Macduff: what need I fear of thee?' (IV.1.81). • Ironically, Macbeth thinks the prophecy will save him.
• There is something impulsive and irrational in Macduff's behaviour.	• 'His flight was madness: when our actions do not,/Our fears do make us traitors' (IV.2.3). • Fear makes him leave his wife and children.
• Macduff is a passionate and true man.	• 'Macduff, this noble passion … thy good truth and honour' (IV.3.114–17). • Malcolm sees he can be trusted.

AIMING HIGH: WRITING ABOUT MACDUFF

Shakespeare shows us two aspects of Macduff's character with his flight to England. He illustrates his 'noble passion' (IV.3.114) and also raises the question of his judgement. Lady Macduff implies that his flight is due to cowardice and Malcolm is initially suspicious of Macduff's motives for leaving Scotland. When writing about Macduff, consider whether his flight was the right thing to do. Are affairs of state more important than family considerations? Is Macduff calculating in a political way? Balance his passion for justice with his flight to England. Did he simply not foresee the extent of savagery that Macbeth would exercise on his family?

THE WITCHES

THE WITCHES' ROLE IN THE PLAY

The witches embody demonic intelligences; they provide information, but do not directly invite human beings to commit crimes. In the play, the witches:

● seem evil and appear to provide information about the future (I.3, IV.1). This destabilises the present by tempting Macbeth.

EXAM FOCUS: WRITING ABOUT THE WITCHES (A01)

Key point	Evidence/Further meaning
● They are presented as agents of evil and are deceptive and dangerous.	● 'And oftentimes to win us to our harm,/The instruments of darkness tell us truths' (I.3.122–3) ● They use truth itself to influence a terrible outcome.
● Their message is compelling and attractive.	● 'Would they had stayed!' (I.3.81) – Macbeth is fascinated by them.
● The witches are infected or diseased and those who trust them will be damned – as Macbeth is.	● 'Infected be the air whereon they ride,/And damned all those that trust them' (IV.1.137–9)
● The witches are controlled by higher supernatural powers.	● 'Call 'em. Let me see 'em' (IV.1.62) ● Macbeth asks the witches to call their masters.

TOP TIP (A02)

Look at film and stage presentations of the witches for different interpretations of these characters. For example compare Roman Polanski's witches with those in the televised version featuring Patrick Stewart.

TOP TIP: WRITING ABOUT THE WITCHES (A01)

When writing about the witches, focus on how Shakespeare presents them: Are they male or female? Can they be said to have human characters? Shakespeare suggests that they embody evil and demonic intelligence. This is fixed and elemental: they do not change, unlike Macbeth. Their information tempts Macbeth – but notice that they do not invite him to murder Duncan or even suggest that he does. Shakespeare  suggests that information is morally neutral until human beings begin to interpret it. Thus the witches symbolise evil, but man is free to resist them. Macbeth is tragic partly because he comes to depend upon their information.

MALCOLM, LADY MACDUFF AND ROSS

THEIR ROLES IN THE PLAY

- **Malcolm** is the son of Duncan and heir to the throne. He fears being falsely framed for murdering Duncan and flees to England. Later he returns with an English army to reclaim the throne
- Malcolm outlines true kingly virtues (IV.3) to Macduff and replaces Macbeth as king
- **Lady Macduff** is the brave wife of Macduff. She does not run away, despite warnings. She is murdered with her son by criminals sent by Macbeth
- Lady Macduff embodies the qualities of a loving mother and wife (IV.2).
- **Ross** is an enigmatic thane who always seems to be on the right side of self-preservation
- Ross brings news (I.3, IV.3), but his motives are often questionable

EXAM FOCUS: WRITING ABOUT MALCOLM, LADY MACDUFF AND ROSS (A01)

Key point	Evidence/Further meaning
● Malcolm, the rightful king, takes the crown in the end.	● 'Hail king, for so thou art' (V.6.93).
● Lady Macduff is loved by her family and friends.	● 'My dearest cuz' (IV.2.15). Ross addresses her with this term of endearment.
● Ross is to attend Macbeth's coronation. He will fit in with the new order.	● 'Well may you see things well done there: adieu.' (II.4.37).

AIMING HIGH: THE ROLE OF MINOR CHARACTERS ★

Consider that the Porter, who appears in Act II Scene 3, is a comic character, with his own special purpose. Shakespeare bends the Porter's language to serve the themes of the play – while simultaneously giving the actor playing Macbeth an opportunity to wash and change clothing before reappearing on stage!

TOP TIP (A01)

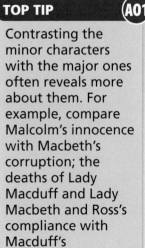

Contrasting the minor characters with the major ones often reveals more about them. For example, compare Malcolm's innocence with Macbeth's corruption; the deaths of Lady Macduff and Lady Macbeth and Ross's compliance with Macduff's stubbornness.

PROGRESS AND REVISION CHECK

SECTION ONE: CHECK YOUR KNOWLEDGE

Answer these quick questions to test your basic knowledge of the play's characters:

1. How is Duncan's leadership different to Macbeth's?
2. How many times does Macbeth meet the witches?
3. What happens to Lady Macbeth after her husband stops confiding in her?
4. How does Banquo die?
5. Who does Malcolm meet with before beginning his attack on Macbeth?
6. Who takes the crown at the end of the play?
7. What does Macbeth wish after the witches disappear?
8. Where does Macduff flee?
9. How does Banquo refer to Macduff?
10. How does Banquo appear at the feast?

SECTION TWO: CHECK YOUR UNDERSTANDING

Here is a task about the role of Duncan. This requires more thought and a slightly longer response. Try to write at least three to four paragraphs.

Task: How does the character of Duncan represent the theme of kingship in the play?

Think about:

- Macbeth's soliloquy in Act I Scene 7 where he presents Duncan's virtues
- Social and historical expectations of kingship – refer to James I

PROGRESS CHECK

GOOD PROGRESS

I can:

- explain the significance of the main characters in how the action develops. ☐
- refer to how they are described by Shakespeare and how this affects the way we see them. ☐

EXCELLENT PROGRESS

I can:

- analyse in detail how Shakespeare has shaped and developed characters over the course of the play. ☐
- infer key ideas, themes and issues from the ways characters and relationships are presented by Shakespeare. ☐

THEMES

AMBITION

Ambition is the fundamental theme and the driving force of Macbeth's life. It is also the theme (in this play) that informs the Shakespearean idea of tragedy. In *Macbeth* the hero's greatest weakness (causing him to fall from grace and inevitably die) is ambition.

- Macbeth acknowledges his 'vaulting ambition' (I.7.27) specifically when he is contemplating the murder of Duncan. This acknowledgement comes after he has considered all the good reasons for not murdering Duncan – only ambition is left to overrule Macbeth's troubled conscience.
- Although the influence of both Lady Macbeth and the witches is strong, their power over Macbeth is only possible because his ambition is already there.
- On first meeting Macbeth we find him startled and fearful of something that sounds 'so fair' (I.3.53). This seems to be because his ambition has already triggered treasonous thoughts.
- Macbeth, then, is a hero but one who is fatally undermined by his ambition. The consequences of this ambition form the fabric of the play.

> **THEME TRACKER (A01)**
>
> **Ambition**
>
> - I.4: Macbeth sees Malcolm as an obstacle.
> - I.7: Macbeth admits to his 'vaulting ambition'.
> - IV.3: Malcolm's ambitions to overthrow Macbeth are revealed.

TOP TIP: WRITING ABOUT CONTRASTING AMBITIONS (A02)

Macbeth and Banquo each receive prophecies from the witches. However, where Banquo is wary of the 'Weird Sisters', Macbeth's ambition is fuelled by their claim that he will become king. When Malcolm is given the title 'Prince of Cumberland' by his father, Macbeth's reaction shows how he sees the natural heir to the throne as an obstacle: 'That is a step/On which I must fall down, or else o'erleap,/ For in my way it lies' (I.4.48–50). When writing about ambition it is important to see that while Banquo may have his own ambitions he does not act on them, whereas Macbeth doggedly pursues his.

Remember too that ambition is also explored through Lady Macbeth, who is similarly inclined. We can contrast their approaches to ambition: she is strong initially while Macbeth wavers, and finally he is strong while she breaks down.

AIMING HIGH: THE ROLE OF FATE ⭐

A key question to ask yourself when writing about *Macbeth* is to what extent Macbeth is responsible for his own downfall? Ambition is undoubtedly Macbeth's fatal flaw, but events are triggered by the witches' prophecies, which suggest that the fates of Macbeth, Macduff and Banquo are already sealed. Which do you think is the more powerful driver in the play – Macbeth's ambition or the hand of Fate? We could argue that a great deal of the tension in the play comes from the clash of these two important forces.

THEME TRACKER (A01)

The Supernatural

- I.1: First appearance of the witches.
- I.3: The witches speak with Macbeth and Banquo.
- II.1: Macbeth sees a dagger.
- III.4: Banquo's ghost.
- III.5: The witches meet with Hecat.
- IV.1 Macbeth summons the witches.

KEY CONTEXT (A03)

King James hated witchcraft. In 1592 he interrogated the witch Agnes Sampson. He was astounded when she privately revealed to him the words he and his wife had spoken in bed together on the first night of their marriage. James 'swore by the living God that he believed all the devils in Hell could not have discovered the same' ('Newes from Scotland 1591' as quoted in J. D. Wilson, *Life in Shakespeare's England: A Book of Elizabethan Prose*, 2008).

THE SUPERNATURAL

The theme of the supernatural appears in the play in various guises – as the witches, as visions and in Lady Macbeth's incantations.

- Witchcraft has four functions in the play: it exposes the evil hiding within Macbeth; it directs his evil to particular deeds; it highlights the forces of evil at work in the world; and it creates a powerful atmosphere in the play.

- The witches only appear in four scenes (I.1, I.3, III.5, IV.1). However, they are the first characters we meet and their evil sets the scene for everything to come: thunder and lightning suggest the havoc that Scotland is about to experience. The witches know they will tell Macbeth something that will prey on his mind. The witches' knowledge is like a drug to Macbeth. He is hooked on them from the start – 'would they had stayed' (I.3.83) – and continually wants more. This leads him to seek them out later. Banquo warns against trusting supernatural knowledge, but Macbeth will not listen.

- Macbeth is particularly affected by the supernatural, with his visions of the dagger (II.1) and Banquo's ghost (III.4).

- When Lady Macbeth calls on the dark forces (I.5) she is asking demonic spirits to possess her mind and body so that all her human pity can be removed.

TOP TIP: WRITING ABOUT THE SUPERNATURAL (A01)

In writing about the supernatural, aim to explore how Shakespeare shows how it affects human beings, but is not in itself responsible for their actions. This is clearly shown by the parallel careers of Banquo and Macbeth: both are tempted by the witches but Banquo resists the temptation to force the prophecy.

AIMING HIGH: CASTING SPELLS ⭐

Notice how the witches often speak in patterns that remind us of magic spells. Unlike other characters, who mostly speak in blank verse, the witches' lines are shorter and often rhyme. At other times they speak chorally, creating the impression that they are one being and adding to their strangeness. At the start of the play they warn that 'Fair is foul, and foul is fair' (I.1.11). This is echoed by Macbeth when we first meet him: 'So foul and fair a day I have not seen' (I.3.37). Do the witches cause the 'foul' atmosphere? Or simply comment on it?

TOP TIP: NATURAL VERSUS SUPERNATURAL (A02)

Notice how Macbeth is fascinated by supernatural revelations, which Banquo rejects – Banquo is a lover of nature (I.4) instead. Shakespeare suggests that the 'supernatural' is in fact the opposite of 'natural', with all kinds of unnatural acts, such as the murder of Macduff's children, happening when Macbeth is king. See **Contexts**.

REVENGE

Revenge is an important **theme** and is contrasted with the idea of justice being done.

- When Duncan asks whether the traitorous Cawdor has been executed (I.4.1), he is asking for justice.
- Macbeth's execution of Duncan's guards is not an example of justice, even though Macbeth claims to act in revenge for Duncan's murder. When Banquo's ghost appears, apparently seeking revenge for his death, Macbeth notes that 'Blood will have blood' (III.4.122).
- Later, when Macbeth summons the witches, the ghost of Banquo 'smiles' (IV.1.123) at him, implying that his revenge is complete and that his descendants will be kings.

Perhaps most importantly of all in terms of the play is Macduff's vengeance. By murdering Macduff's family Macbeth sets against himself the one man who can defeat him. Macduff's mission for revenge is entirely personal – he promises that Macbeth escaping from him is as likely as heaven forgiving him (IV.3.233–4).

TOP TIP: WRITING ABOUT PATTERNS OF REVENGE (A01)

Examine the pattern of this theme by looking at the blood relatives who are affected by Macbeth's actions. Malcolm and Donalbain lose their father to Macbeth, as does Fleance, and the sons want revenge. The sons of Macduff and Old Seyward are killed and so the fathers will also seek retribution. 'It will have blood; they say, blood will have blood' (III.4.122) Macbeth hopes that murdering Duncan can be the 'be-all' and 'end-all' (I.7.5) of the matter but revenge is not so easily set aside.

THEME TRACKER (A01)

Revenge

- I.4: The Thane of Cawdor is executed for treason.
- II.3: Macbeth murders the chamberlains.
- IV.3: Malcolm encourages Macduff to seek revenge for his family.

KEY CONTEXT (A03)

The fall of the Earl of Essex during the reign of Elizabeth I happened only five years prior to *Macbeth* being written. Essex was perceived as being ambitious. To what extent might this real life event have influenced Shakespeare?

THEME TRACKER **A01**

Kingship

- I.2: We first meet King Duncan

- I.7: Macbeth describes Duncan's popularity

- IV.1: The witches show Macbeth a line of eight kings

KINGSHIP

The theme of kingship is important and the play presents examples of good and bad rule in the form of Duncan and Macbeth.

- Duncan is presented as a just and fair king. He rewards his men with honours and makes Macbeth Thane of Cawdor.
- When Macbeth contemplates killing Duncan in Act I Scene 7 he lists Duncan's virtues.
- Macbeth comes to be king through immoral means and his rule continues in this way.
- When Duncan is fair, Macbeth is tyrannical and becomes murderous. His rule is a brutal dictatorship.
- Edward is King of England and, in contrast to Macbeth, is portrayed as a good king, well-liked by his people.
- Malcolm, Duncan's son, is crowned King at the end of the play.

HOLINSHED'S *CHRONICLES*

The story of Macbeth is based on historical events as depicted in Holinshed's *Chronicles of England, Scotland and Ireland*. Macbeth and Banquo feature in these chronicles as warriors who meet with 'thrée women in strange and wild apparell'. In these histories, it is Macbeth and Banquo, rather than Lady Macbeth, who murder King Duncan.

KEY CONTEXT: THE GREAT CHAIN OF BEING **A03**

In Shakespeare's time people believed that authority was derived from God in a great chain of being. God was at the top then came angels, mankind, animals, birds, fish and so on. In the human order the king was supreme. Males were above females. Thus, questioning the will of the king had religious as well as political significance.

CONTEXTS

SHAKESPEARE'S LIFE

William Shakespeare was born in Stratford-upon-Avon in 1564 and he died there almost exactly fifty-two years later, in 1616. During those fifty-two years he created at least thirty-seven plays and possibly had a hand in others. He also wrote poems, including more than 150 sonnets.

KING JAMES I OF ENGLAND

Macbeth was written some time between 1603 and 1606. This coincides with the accession of James the Sixth of Scotland to the English throne, as James the First of England, in 1603. The playwright certainly seemed to have James in mind whilst writing.

The play appeals to many of the king's interests: it echoes his fascination with the supernatural (witches and prophecies); it compliments him by making his ancestor, Banquo, a hero in the play (IV.1). King James had survived an assassination attempt, so the questions about the role of the monarchy and the duties of their subjects that this play explored would have been pertinent to Shakespeare's original audience.

SUCCESSION AND ORDER

Of great importance in Shakespeare's time was the political issue of succession (deciding who would be the next king or queen). Elizabeth, who preceded James I, remained the 'Virgin' Queen throughout her reign, which meant she had no natural successor. This created instability in the country. Elizabeth did not name her successor until she was on her deathbed.

Rebellion and anarchy had to be avoided in future – hence the importance of order, 'degree' (rank) and loyalty. We see a reference to this at Macbeth's feast when he invites his assembled guests to sit down: 'You know your own degrees' (III.4.1). Where one sat was determined by rank. The king ruled over men by divine appointment and to violate or seek to violate this situation was against God's will, and would produce 'unnatural' results. The unnatural killing of Duncan is accompanied by, among other things, 'A falcon [a royal bird] towering in her pride of place', which is 'by a mousing owl [an inferior bird] hawked at, and killed' (II.4.12–13).

> **KEY CONTEXT** (A03)
>
> The Porter alludes to the topical events of the Gunpowder Plot of 1605 and the subsequent trials of its conspirators (II.3). Research these events and write a list of connections between them and the play.

SETTINGS

SETTING AND PLACE

The play is set mostly in Scotland, apart from IV.3 where Macduff joins Malcolm in England. The action takes place either outdoors – the witches on the heath, the murder of Banquo, the English army advancing – or within castle walls – the planning to murder Duncan, the murder of Duncan, the murder of Lady Macduff, the sleep walking of Lady Macbeth and so on. This gives the play two contrasting qualities: outdoors there is an elemental sense of force and nature; within the castle there is a sense of claustrophobic evil.

KEY CONTEXT (A03)

Shakespeare uses the darkness to symbolically remind his audience of Christ's crucifixion and the great darkness that the Bible says enveloped the land after Christ's death.

AIMING HIGH: WRITING ABOUT SETTING AND PLACE ⭐

Macbeth is a play – a fiction – but one of the reasons that it seems so realistic and compelling is its use of setting and place. The castles – true to their military origins – become places of bloodshed and suffering: Duncan is murdered in Macbeth's castle; later Macbeth defends the realm and is killed outside his own castle; Macduff's family is slaughtered in their home at Fife. On the other hand, Scone, where Macbeth is crowned, is a holy place. Add to this the place names – Birnan Wood (and Dunsinane) – that occur in the prophecies, and we can sense a kind of life or death force in each of these locations.

REVISION FOCUS: MAKE SURE YOU KNOW THE PLOT 🕐

Draw a timeline for the play with sketches or images of each of the key locations and where they occur in the plot alongside each scene. This will provide you with a visual idea of the change of mood and tone as the play progresses.

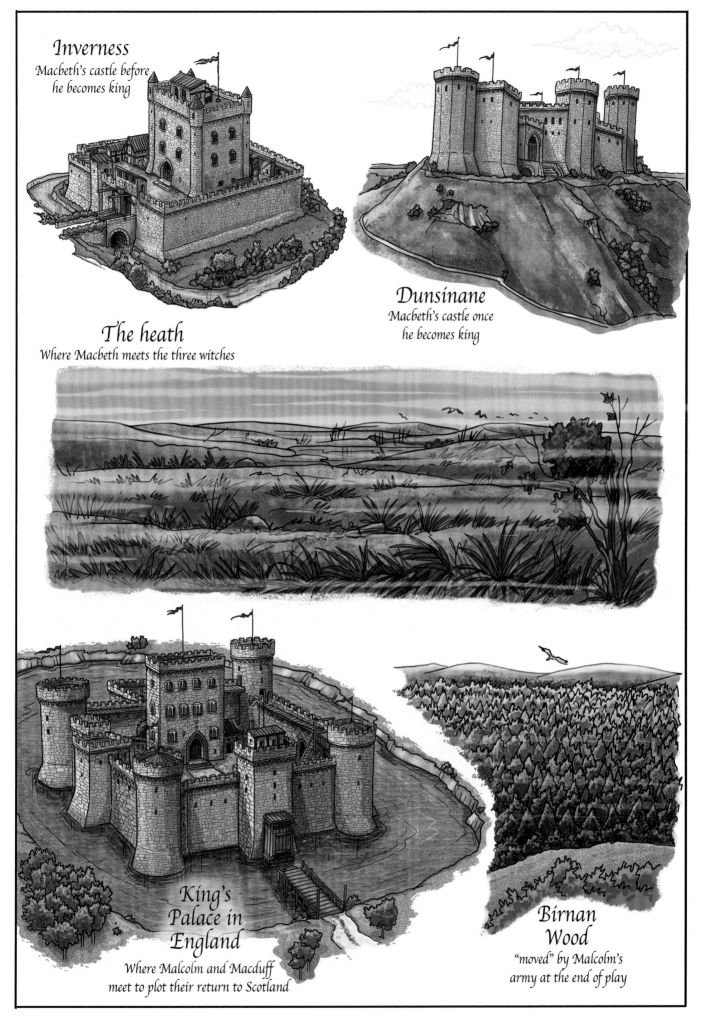

Inverness
Macbeth's castle before he becomes king

Dunsinane
Macbeth's castle once he becomes king

The heath
Where Macbeth meets the three witches

King's Palace in England
Where Malcolm and Macduff meet to plot their return to Scotland

Birnan Wood
"moved" by Malcolm's army at the end of play

PROGRESS AND REVISION CHECK

SECTION ONE: CHECK YOUR KNOWLEDGE

Answer these quick questions to test your basic knowledge of the themes, contexts and settings of the play:

1. Which key theme is also Macbeth's driving force?

2. Whose revenge results directly in Macbeth's final downfall?

3. Which line spoken by the witches does Macbeth later echo?

4. Who was king of England at the time this play was written?

5. Which characters are associated with the heath?

6. Who wrote the *Chronicles of England, Scotland and Ireland*?

7. How many scenes do the witches appear in?

8. Who, apart from Macbeth, receives prophecies from the witches?

9. Which brothers are affected by Macbeth's actions?

10. Who is presented as a just and honest king?

SECTION TWO: CHECK YOUR UNDERSTANDING

Here is a task about the theme of ambition. This requires more thought and a slightly longer response. Try to write at least three to four paragraphs.

How is the theme of ambition presented in *Macbeth*?

Think about:

- Lady Macbeth's ambition as well as Macbeth's
- How Banquo responds to his ambition differently from Macbeth

PROGRESS CHECK

GOOD PROGRESS

I can:

- explain the main themes, contexts and settings in the text and how they contribute to the effect on the reader. ☐
- use a range of appropriate evidence to support any points I make about these elements. ☐

EXCELLENT PROGRESS

I can:

- analyse in detail the way themes are developed and presented across the play. ☐
- refer closely to key aspects of context and setting and the implications they have for the writer's viewpoint, and the interpretation of relationships and ideas. ☐

FORM

OVERVIEW

Macbeth takes the form of a play. However, as a play by Shakespeare, perhaps the most famous English dramatist, it also has some special characteristics, which are shared with his other dramatic works. Form refers to the shared characteristics a particular text has.

A PLAY

As a play, *Macbeth* is made up completely of dialogue: words spoken by the characters to each other that present us with the story or plot. Dialogue is designed to be delivered by actors, performing in a theatre space, for a live audience.

A SHAKESPEARE PLAY

A Shakespeare play has many conventions of its own which reflect the time in which it was written, a time when there was a great appetite for going to the theatre and watching plays.

They are presented in five separate acts for example and were written mainly in verse rather than prose. Whilst we do not know whether Shakespeare himself divided the plays in this way, the editors who collected his works decided that this helped understand their structure.

Shakespeare was a very inventive dramatist and wrote thirty-seven plays of many different types. He wrote plays that were based on history, plays that were comedies, and plays, such as *Macbeth*, that were tragedies.

AIMING HIGH: TRAGEDY

A tragedy is a form of classical drama, most closely associated with the Ancient Greeks and Romans. It presents tragic events: ones that deal with suffering, loss and death. Traditionally a tragedy would deal with the downfall of one, usually very important, or high status character. It would have what is known as a unity, in that it would deal with one main **plot**, in a single location, or place, and in a time span of twenty-four hours.

We can see how Shakespeare uses this structure in *Macbeth* where the protagonist rises to power, and as a result of his fatal flaw of ambition, loses everything. The play is mainly set in Macbeth's castle, and has a single plot.

TOP TIP (A02)

Look out for deliberate structural parallels. Just as Lady Macduff runs off stage screaming to her death in Act IV Scene 2, so in Act V Scene 5 Lady Macbeth screams off stage as she takes her own life. In Lady Macbeth's case, Macbeth hears it. The train of events he has started effectively return to his own family, as Shakespeare makes clear with this use of parallel action.

STRUCTURE

TOP TIP (A02)

Structure can also refer to the way that a writer constructs the text. Shakespeare constructs the play using the building blocks of prose and poetry. Most of his work is written in blank verse, but sometimes characters speak in rhyme or prose too, for different effects.

OVERVIEW

Shakespeare uses many different means to structure *Macbeth*. Structure refers to the different methods a writer uses to add shape and organisation to a text. The structure of *Macbeth* helps us to keep track of events and follow the action with understanding. Other structural methods that Shakespeare uses add variety to the play and add to its tension and excitement.

A SINGLE PLOT

Macbeth is Shakespeare's shortest tragedy. One reason for this is that there is no subplot. All the action contributes to the central focus on Macbeth himself. This creates – as befits the intensity of evil in the play – a unified and powerful effect. The play itself has the traditional five Acts, which are then subdivided into scenes. Whilst we do not know whether Shakespeare himself divided the plays in this way, the editors who collected his works decided that this helped understand their structure. Within that framework the structure is twofold: we see the rise of Macbeth to power, and we see his fall. Both activities are prefaced by the witches' contributions.

RISE AND FALL: A TWOFOLD STRUCTURE

- In Acts I and II Macbeth rises to a position of power.
- The turning point is in Act III at the banquet scene when Macbeth has achieved the full limit and splendour of his power. At this point the thanes of Scotland (apart from Macduff) are prepared to accept him. However, the murder of Banquo produces catastrophic consequences implied by the way the ghost takes Macbeth's chair.
- Following this event Macbeth decides to revisit the witches, and from here onwards his power declines and his depravity increases.

TOP TIP (A01)

Try watching the 1997 film version of *Macbeth* starring Jason Connery and Helen Baxendale. Are there any changes that have been made to the structure of the play, e.g. scenes omitted, or events taking place in different order? What effect does this have on the story?

In this twofold structure Shakespeare first reflects the idea of crime and consequence. Macbeth comments on the dangers of 'even-handed justice' (I.7.10) and this proves true in terms of the play's structure: what he does in the first half of the play returns to haunt him in the second half.

Second, Shakespeare shows how the characters of Macbeth and Lady Macbeth pivot round the twofold structure: it is Lady Macbeth who exults in evil until the middle point of the play, and her husband who is fearful of the damnable consequences; after the assassination of Banquo these positions are reversed.

This point about a twofold structure should not surprise us when we reflect upon the essential nature of the play: it is about good versus evil, and 'foul' being 'fair' (I.1.11). These oppositions and contrasts run through the whole play.

BLANK VERSE

What is blank verse?	Shakespeare often writes unrhymed lines in iambic pentameter. This is **blank verse** and is the poetic medium in which most of the play is written.
Example	'Your face, my thane, is as a book where men May read strange matters. To beguile the time' (I.5.60–1).
Effect	The most important words are stressed: face, thane, book, time. The stress gives greater prominence to key ideas and adds another layer of richness to the meanings of words.

Iambic pentameter mirrors the patterns and rhythm of natural speech. One iambic foot consists of two syllables, the first one unstressed, the second stressed. For example 'Mac<u>beth</u>' is an iamb. There are five iambic feet in iambic pentameter.

Shakespeare's mastery of blank verse is renowned. He uses the form to create realistic characters for the audience. He also uses blank verse to give greater prominence to key ideas and to add another layer of richness to the meanings of words.

TOP TIP: WRITING ABOUT BLANK VERSE (A02)

It is often most interesting to notice when the conventions of blank verse are broken and to question why. For example in Act II Scene 1 Macbeth hears the bell ringing – his sign to commence the plot to murder his king. He says '<u>Hear</u> it <u>not</u>, Duncan, for <u>it</u> is a <u>knell</u>' (line 63). Notice how the first word of this line is stressed rather than the second. This disturbance to the iambic pentameter reflects Macbeth's anxiety. It could be said to echo a sudden fluttering of heartbeat.

PROSE

What is prose?	Prose is language that is without a specific pattern or metre.
Example	The Porter, in the only vaguely comic scene in the play, speaks in prose: 'Knock, knock! Who's there in the other devil's name?' (II.3.7).
Effect	The move from blank verse signifies a change in tone from seriousness to humour.

Shakespeare uses prose in several scenes, most notably in the letter to Lady Macbeth (I.5), the Porter scene (II.3), the murder of Lady Macduff and her son (IV.2) and Lady Macbeth's sleep walking scene (V.1). In each case prose signifies a different atmosphere and often refers to heightened or disturbed emotions.

TOP TIP (A02)

The Porter, like many of Shakespeare's characters with lower social standing, speaks in prose. Blank verse is more 'noble' and generally reserved for nobler characters. This suggests that when high-ranking characters speak in prose it indicates a falling away from nobility. Lady Macduff begins by speaking in blank verse but as the pressure on her increases prose takes over. She regains the power of blank verse – and so dignity – as she confronts the murderers.

TOP TIP (A02)

Shakespeare frequently concludes a scene with a rhyming couplet. This often points to a central idea. For example, Macbeth says that the bell, for Duncan, rings for heaven or hell: 'The bell invites me. / Hear it not, Duncan – for it is a knell / That summons thee to heaven or to hell' (II.1.63–5). The word 'hell' is afforded extra resonance and depth because of the rhyme. The simple monosyllabic rhyme of 'bell', 'knell' and 'hell' also reflects the sound of the ringing bell.

TOP TIP (A04)

When exploring imagery in the text, you will notice how Shakespeare uses simile and metaphor. For example, Duncan compares the quality of nobleness to stars when he says 'signs of nobleness, like stars, shall shine / On all deservers' (I.4.42–3). Consider what this comparison says about nobleness.

RHYME

What is rhyme?	Rhyme is the use of words with similar sounds, such as 'bell', 'knell' and 'hell'. Rhyming couplets are pairs of lines with end words that form perfect rhymes.
Example	The last two lines of the play are a rhyming couplet: 'So thanks to all at once, and to each one,/Whom we invite to see us crowned at Scone.' (V.6.113–4).
Effect	This rhyming couplet signifies a final end to the drama.

Shakespeare mainly uses rhyming couplets in *Macbeth* to show the end of a scene. He also uses them for the witches to suggest the world of spells and incantations:

> 'Fillet of a fenny snake,
> In the cauldron boil and bake –
> Eye of newt, and toe of frog,
> Wool of bat and tongue of dog,'

(IV.1.12–19)

Notice that the witches do not speak in iambic pentameter. Their lines are more often eight syllables in length and follow a pattern that is the opposite of iambic meter: stressed then unstressed (this is called trochaic tetrameter). This different speech pattern makes the witches seem even stranger than other characters.

LANGUAGE

OVERVIEW

Shakespeare is renowned for his use of language, for his mastery of original and striking images that have stood the test of time. The language of his plays is beautiful, clever and highly poetical.

LANGUAGE DEVICE: IMAGERY

What is imagery?	Imagery is language that is visually descriptive or figurative.
Example	The captain uses violent imagery to describe Macbeth's actions in battle. He tells us that 'brave Macbeth...unseamed [Macdonwald] from the nave to the chops' (I.2.22).
Effect	This presents the audience with the fearless and ferocious character of Macbeth before they meet him.

Shakespeare uses imagery to give his plays depth and resonance. You will find examples of imagery in most scenes and should consider the relevance of the images presented. Consider how an image works to reveal more about a character or theme. For example, in Act I Scene 5 we are presented with the image of Lady Macbeth calling on the spirits of darkness: 'Come, you spirits' (I.5.38). She asks them to 'Make thick my blood' (I.5.41), which suggests she wants to become stronger. The image of blood also suggests the violence that is to follow.

AIMING HIGH: WRITING ABOUT IMAGERY

Remember to comment on how Shakespeare uses words, sometimes literal, sometimes figurative, to create, through their associations, the rich imagery of the play: blood, dark, light, feasting, clothing and children. Because these words and ideas are constantly being explored and exploited, the effect is to create a wealth of nuances and meanings, ambiguities and insights.

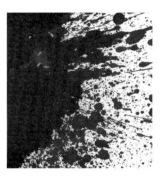

LANGUAGE DEVICE: MOTIF

What is a motif?	A motif is a repeated idea or image used throughout a text.
Example	Duncan is murdered while he sleeps, and in committing this act of treason, Macbeth ironically 'does murder sleep' (II.2.36).
Effect	This re-emphasises the repeated image of 'sleep' that runs through *Macbeth*, and links it to murder.

Shakespeare uses some images repeatedly to emphasise their importance to the meaning of the play. These motifs create a dense texture. In *Macbeth* two of the most significant motifs are those of blood and sleep. These combine in Act V when the doctor observes Lady Macbeth's mental and emotional breakdown manifesting in her sleepwalking. She is obsessed with a 'damned spot' (V.1.34) of blood that she cannot wash from her hands. Both the blood and her disturbed sleep represent her guilt.

REVISION FOCUS: WRITING ABOUT MOTIFS

Keep a track of where each motif occurs throughout the play. Select one example and explore the implications of it. Then compare that to a later occurrence of the motif. For example, in Act II Scene 2, Lady Macbeth orders her husband to 'smear/The sleepy grooms with blood' (II.2.48–9). Compare this to Act V when she is desperate to remove the blood from herself.

LANGUAGE DEVICE: REPETITION

What is repetition?	Repetition is the use of the same, or similar, words throughout a text
Example	Words like 'done', 'won', 'lost', 'fair', 'foul' are repeated in *Macbeth*.
Effect	By repeating these words throughout they are given increasing significance in the play.

TOP TIP A02

Listen to an audio version of a key speech from the play. Listen to the emphasis that the actor puts on certain words, then try reading the same speech out loud yourself. This can help you to understand and appreciate how Shakespeare's language works.

If we take just one of these words, 'done', and examine a few of its appearances we get some idea of how important repetition is:

- It first appears in Act I: 'When the hurly-burly's done,/When the battle's lost and won' (I.1.3–4).
- We find the word again in the next scene. Ross says, 'I'll see it done' and Duncan replies, ending the scene (see Shakespeare's use of **rhyming couplets**), 'What he hath lost, noble Macbeth hath won' (I.2.69–70).
- Later, Duncan asks, 'Is execution done on Cawdor?' (I.4.1) and by Scene 5 of the first Act Lady Macbeth is saying: 'That which cries "Thus thou must do" if thou have it – / And that which rather thou dost fear to do,/ Than wishest should be undone' (I.5.22–4).

Doing and not-doing – simple ideas and words as they are – clearly relate people to their eternal destiny, as well as the outcomes of this life: winning and losing. Ironically the sense of being 'undone' is never far from such 'doing' in the case of Macbeth.

LANGUAGE DEVICE: SYMBOLISM

What is symbolism?	Symbolism means the use of symbols or images to represent ideas, themes or characteristics.
Example	The serpent is a symbol used to represent treachery. Lady Macbeth warns her husband to 'look like the innocent flower,/But be the serpent under't' (I.5.63–4).
Effect	The symbolism here shows that Lady Macbeth wishes her husband to appear well-meaning and gentle to hide his deceit. The symbol also has connotations of temptation and lost innocence through the serpent's link to the biblical story of Adam and Eve.

The symbolism of the play is connected with the imagery: blood, for example, operates on at least four levels – Donalbain refers to 'near in blood' (II.3.136) to signify family. Blood is also what is literally shed when wars and murders occur; it is part of the imagery that pervades the play, creating a sense of menace and destruction; and it is a symbol for the evil that is associated with Macbeth.

TOP TIP WRITING ABOUT BIBLICAL IMAGERY (A02)

It is important in terms of the symbols to remember the Christian and biblical context in which the play was written. Even Macbeth acknowledges heaven and hell, and the references to light and dark. The great Christian symbols – the crucifixion, for example – are not only events from the Bible, but also are symbolic, and have parallels in *Macbeth*.

We might like to think of Duncan as the innocent and good (Christ-like) king who is betrayed by one of his followers (or disciples), Macbeth. This, of course, parallels Judas Iscariot's betrayal of Christ. As you study the play, you may detect even more parallels – for example, the darkness surrounding the crucifixion, and the darkness on the night of the murder of Duncan.

PROGRESS AND REVISION CHECK

SECTION ONE: CHECK YOUR KNOWLEDGE

Answer these quick questions to test your basic knowledge of the form, structure and language of the play:

1 Which character speaks in prose?

2 How many syllables are in a line of iambic pentameter?

3 What type of structure does this play follow?

4 Which characters speak in rhyming couplets?

5 Name one motif in *Macbeth*.

6 Which Acts show Macbeth's rise to power?

7 What genre does this play belong to?

8 What is the name given to a repeated idea of an image in a text?

9 How many Acts are in the play altogether?

10 What term describes the main character in a play?

SECTION TWO: CHECK YOUR UNDERSTANDING

Here is a task about the motif of sleep. This requires more thought and a slightly longer response. Try to write at least three to four paragraphs.

How does Shakespeare use the motif of sleep in *Macbeth*?

Think about:

● Macbeth's concern that he has murdered sleep after he kills Duncan
● How Lady Macbeth is tormented by sleeplessness

PROGRESS CHECK

GOOD PROGRESS

I can:

● explain how the writer uses form, structure and language to develop the action, show relationships, and develop ideas. ☐

● use relevant quotations to support the points I make, and make reference to the effect of some language choices. ☐

EXCELLENT PROGRESS

I can:

● analyse in detail Shakespeare's use of particular forms, structures and language techniques to convey ideas, create characters, and evoke mood or setting. ☐

● select from a range of evidence, including apt quotations, to infer the effect of particular language choices, and to develop wider interpretations. ☐

UNDERSTANDING THE QUESTION

For your exam, you will be answering an extract-based question and/or a question on the whole of *Macbeth*. Check with your teacher to see what sort of question you are doing. Whatever the task, questions in exams will need **decoding.** This means highlighting and understanding the key words so that the answer you write is relevant.

BREAK DOWN THE QUESTION

Pick out the **key words** or phrases. For example:

Read the following extract from Act I Scene 5, starting 'If we should fail?' to 'false heart doth know'.

Question: How does Shakespeare **present** the **theme of deceit** through **the character of Lady Macbeth** in **this extract** and in the **play as a whole?**

What does this tell you?

- Focus on **the theme of deceit** and also on **Lady Macbeth.**
- The word **'present'** tells you to examine the ways Shakespeare shows this theme.
- The phrases 'this extract' and 'play as a whole' mean you need to **start** with the given **extract** and then **widen your discussion** to the rest of the play, but sticking to the theme **in both.**

TOP TIP (A01)

You might be asked to 'refer closely to', which means picking out specific examples from the play, or to focus on 'methods and techniques', which mean the 'things' Shakespeare does, for example, the use of a particular language feature, an ironic comment on an event, etc.

PLANNING YOUR ANSWER

It is vital that you generate ideas quickly, and plan your answer efficiently when you sit the exam. Stick to your plan, and with a timer to hand; tick off each part as you progress.

STAGE 1: GENERATE IDEAS QUICKLY

Very briefly **list your key ideas** based on the question you have **decoded.** For example:

- In the **extract** Lady Macbeth outlines her plan to blame the guards for Duncan's murder, saying that drink will deceive them.
- Shakespeare uses rhetorical language to present her as persuasively deceptive.
- In the **play as a whole** Lady Macbeth tells her husband to act innocently, even though their plans are evil.
- Macbeth later arranges for Banquo to be murdered without consulting his wife – deceiving his friend and his partner.
- Lady Macbeth is connected with the witches, who could also be accused of deceit, with their ambiguous prophecies.
- Macbeth becomes deceitful and does not tell her the details of his plan to murder Banquo. Deceit contributes to the breakdown of their relationship.
- The armies march on Dunsinane, disguised with branches from Birnan Wood – another example of deceit.

STAGE 2: JOT DOWN USEFUL QUOTATIONS (OR KEY EVENTS)

For example, from the **extract**:

'Who dares receive it other,/As we shall make our griefs and clamour roar/Upon his death?'

From the **play as a whole**:

Lady Macbeth, Act I Scene 5: 'look like the innocent flower,/But be the serpent under't.'

STAGE 3: PLAN FOR PARAGRAPHS

Use paragraphs to plan your answer. Remember to comment on language and to include social and historical context. For example:

Paragraph	Point
Paragraph 1	**Introduce** the **argument** you wish to make. *In this scene we see Lady Macbeth persuading Macbeth to go through with her deceitful plan to murder Duncan. She uses vivid imagery and persuasive language to manipulate her husband.*
Paragraph 2	Your first point: *She plans to give the chamberlains so much wine that they will be unable to defend themselves. You could comment on the image of 'spongy officers' and focus on layers of meaning – they will absorb the drink she plies them with and also soak up the blame.*
Paragraph 3	Your second point: *She says that no one will question the Macbeths if they pretend they are shocked and grieving when they hear the news of Duncan's death. She uses a rhetorical question to challenge the idea that anyone would doubt the 'roar' of their grief.*
Paragraph 4	Your third point: *Macbeth is persuaded by her plan and agrees to accept this 'false' behaviour. Lady Macbeth had prepared him for this in Act I Scene 5 when she said they would have to act innocently.*
Paragraph 5	Your fourth point: *Deceit is not rewarded in this play and we see how the Macbeths ultimately break down as a result of their cunning behaviour. Their relationship is weakened and Lady Macbeth seems to mentally fall apart. In the play as a whole we also see deceit in the form of the witches' prophecies. These are ambiguous and are misinterpreted by Macbeth. There is also the plot to usurp Macbeth, could be seen as deceitful. The soldiers use branches to disguise themselves as they march on Dunsinane.* [You may want to add further paragraphs if you have time]
Conclusion	**Sum up** your argument: *In conclusion, deceit leads to further acts of deception in this play. The initial crime of murdering Duncan spirals and turns on itself so Macbeth is even deceitful towards his wife.*

TOP TIP   (A02)

When discussing Shakespeare's language, make sure you refer to the techniques he uses, and, most importantly, the *effect* of those techniques. Do not just say, 'Shakespeare uses lots of persuasive language', instead write, 'Shakespeare's use of rhetorical questions in this section shows/emphasises/conveys the idea that … '

RESPONDING TO WRITERS' EFFECTS

The two most important assessment objectives are **AO1** and **AO2**. They are about *what* writers do (the choices they make, and the effects these create), *what* your ideas are (your analysis and interpretation), and *how* you write about them (how well you explain your ideas).

ASSESSMENT OBJECTIVE 1

What does it say?	What does it mean?	Dos and Don'ts
Read, understand and respond to texts. Students should be able to: ● Maintain a critical style and develop an informed personal response ● Use textual references, including quotations, to support and illustrate interpretations	You must: ● Use some of the literary terms you have learned (correctly!) ● Write in a professional way (not a sloppy, chatty way) ● Show you have thought for yourself ● Back up your ideas with examples, including quotations	**Don't write …** *Lady Macbeth is a really evil character. Shakespeare uses lots of forceful words to describe her. Macbeth says she should 'Bring forth men-children only'* **Do write …** *Shakespeare presents Lady Macbeth at the start of the play as a determined, and forceful character. For example Macbeth says she should 'Bring forth men-children only', which implies that she has a strong and ruthless nature with the masculine attributes worthy of a warrior.*

IMPROVING YOUR CRITICAL STYLE

Use a variety of words and phrases to show effects. For example:

Shakespeare *suggests … , conveys … , implies … , explores … , demonstrates … , describes how … , shows how …*

I/we (as readers) *infer … , recognise … , understand … , question … , see … , are given … , reflect …*

For example, look at these two alternative paragraphs by different students about Lady Macbeth. Note the difference in the quality of expression:

Student A:

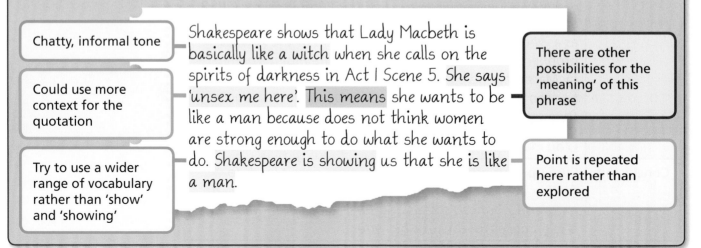

Chatty, informal tone

Could use more context for the quotation

Try to use a wider range of vocabulary rather than 'show' and 'showing'

Shakespeare shows that Lady Macbeth is basically like a witch when she calls on the spirits of darkness in Act I Scene 5. She says 'unsex me here'. This means she wants to be like a man because does not think women are strong enough to do what she wants to do. Shakespeare is showing us that she is like a man.

There are other possibilities for the 'meaning' of this phrase

Point is repeated here rather than explored

Student B:

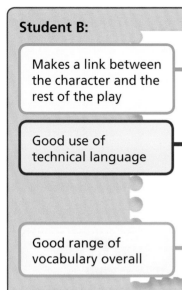

Makes a link between the character and the rest of the play

Good use of technical language

Good range of vocabulary overall

Shakespeare connects Lady Macbeth with the forces of evil in the play when she calls on the spirits of darkness in Act I Scene 5. Her language is commanding: 'Come, you spirits'. The imperative 'Come' could suggest she has some control over the spirits, or alternatively show that she is pleading. She then asks them to 'unsex me here'. This implies that Lady Macbeth regards her own female nature to be a hindrance to her plans.

Specific point about language

Variety of vocabulary for analysis

ASSESSMENT OBJECTIVE 2

What does it say?	What does it mean?	Dos and don'ts
Analyse the language, form and structure used by the writer to create meanings and effects, using relevant subject terminology where appropriate.	'Analyse' – comment **in detail** on **particular aspects** of the text or language. 'Language' – vocabulary, imagery, variety of sentences, dialogue/speech etc. 'Form' – how the story is told (e.g. first person narrative, letters, diaries, chapter by chapter?) 'Structure' – the order in which events are revealed, or in which characters appear, or descriptions are presented. 'Create meaning' – what can we, as readers, infer from what the writer tells us? What is implied by particular descriptions, or events? 'Subject terminology' – words you should use when writing about plays, such as 'character', 'protagonist', 'imagery', 'staging', etc.	**Don't write:** *The witches speak in rhyme, which means we can imagine how they say it.* **Do write:** *Shakespeare **conveys** a sense of unease to the audience through the **rhyme patterns** used by the witches. Unlike other characters who speak in **blank verse**, the witches are distinguished by the spell-like rhythm and rhyme of their speech.*

THE THREE 'I'S

- Firstly, the best analysis focuses on specific ideas, events or uses of language and thinks about what is **implied.**
- This means looking beyond the obvious and beginning to draw **inferences.** On the one hand Macbeth is presented as a brave warrior at the start of the play – but what do we learn about his potential for ruthless brutality, or about his ambitious nature?
- From the inferences you make across the text as a whole, you can arrive at your own **interpretation** – a sense of the bigger picture, a wider evaluation of a person, relationship or idea.

USING QUOTATIONS

One of the secrets of success in writing exam essays is to use quotations **effectively**. There are five basic principles:

1. Only quote what is most useful.
2. Do not use a quotation that repeats what you have just written.
3. Put quotation marks, e.g. ' ', around the quotation.
4. Write the quotation exactly as it appears in the original.
5. Use the quotation so that it fits neatly into your sentence.

EXAM FOCUS: USING QUOTATIONS (A01)

Quotations should be used to develop the line of thought in your essay and 'zoom in' on key details, such as language choices. The example below shows a clear and effective way of doing this:

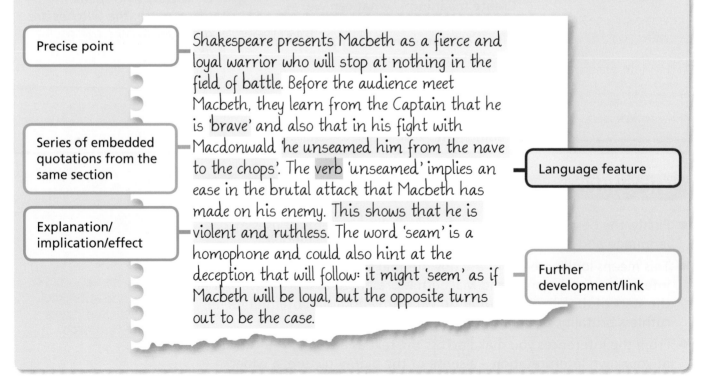

> **Point** — Shakespeare presents Macbeth as a fierce warrior. Before we meet Macbeth, the Captain describes how he fought with the rebel Macdonwald and **'unseamed him from the nave to the chops'** [**Quotation**]. This gruesome depiction of battle shows Macbeth can be ruthless and violent. [**Explanation/effect**]

However, really **high-level responses** will go further. They will make an even more precise point, support it with an even more appropriate quotation, focus in on particular words and phrases and explain the effect or what is implied to make a wider point or draw inferences. Here is an example:

> **Precise point** — Shakespeare presents Macbeth as a fierce and loyal warrior who will stop at nothing in the field of battle. Before the audience meet Macbeth, they learn from the Captain that he is 'brave' and also that in his fight with Macdonwald **'he unseamed him from the nave to the chops'** [**Series of embedded quotations from the same section**]. The verb 'unseamed' [**Language feature**] implies an ease in the brutal attack that Macbeth has made on his enemy. This shows that he is violent and ruthless. [**Explanation/implication/effect**] The word 'seam' is a homophone and could also hint at the deception that will follow: it might 'seem' as if Macbeth will be loyal, but the opposite turns out to be the case. [**Further development/link**]

SPELLING, PUNCTUATION AND GRAMMAR

SPELLING

Remember to spell correctly the **author's** name, the names of all the **characters**, and the **names of places**.

A good idea is to list some of the key spellings you know you sometimes get wrong *before* the exam starts. Then use it to check as you go along. Sometimes it is easy to make small errors as you write but if you have your key word list nearby you can check against it.

PUNCTUATION

Remember:

- Use full stops and commas in sentences accurately to make clear points. Don't write long, rambling sentences that don't make sense; equally, avoid using a lot of short repetitive ones. Write in a fluent way, using linking words and phrases and use inverted commas for quotations.

Don't write	Do write:
At the start of the play we see Macbeth and Banquo together as friends. They meet the witches. Banquo becomes suspicious. Macbeth has him killed.	*At the start of the play Macbeth and Banquo are presented as friends, **though** this bond is challenged by Macbeth's response to the witches. When Banquo becomes suspicious of Macbeth, his jealous friend sends murderers to kill him and his son.*

GRAMMAR

When you are writing about the text, make sure you:

- Use the present tense for discussing what the writer does.
- Use pronouns and references back to make your writing flow.

Don't write	Do write:
Whilst Macbeth was initially presented as a brave and loyal soldier, Macbeth's betrayal of King Duncan showed that Macbeth is ruled by Macbeth's ambition.	*Whilst Macbeth **is** initially presented as a brave and loyal soldier, **his** betrayal of King Duncan **shows** that **he** is ruled by his ambition.*

TOP TIP (A04)

Remember that spelling, punctuation and grammar is worth **5%** of your overall marks, which could mean the difference between one grade and another.

TOP TIP (A04)

Practise your spellings of key literature terms you might use when writing about the text such as: *ironic, dramatic irony, simile, metaphor, imagery, protagonist, character, theme, rhetorical question,* etc.

TOP TIP (A04)

Enliven your essay by varying the way your sentences begin. For example: *Macbeth is persuaded by his wife to murder Duncan, even though he has come to the conclusion that this is not the best course of action,* can also be written as: *Even though Macbeth has come to the conclusion that it is not the best course of action, he is persuaded by his wife to murder Duncan.*

ANNOTATED SAMPLE ANSWERS

This section provides three sample responses, one at **mid** level, one at a **good** level and one at a **very high** level.

> **Question**: In this scene, Macbeth has just returned from killing Duncan.
>
> Read from 'Methoughts I heard a voice cry, "Sleep no more..."' to 'Look on't again, I dare not' (Act II Scene 2).
>
> *Write about how Shakespeare explores ideas about guilt in this extract, and in the play as a whole.*

SAMPLE ANSWER 1

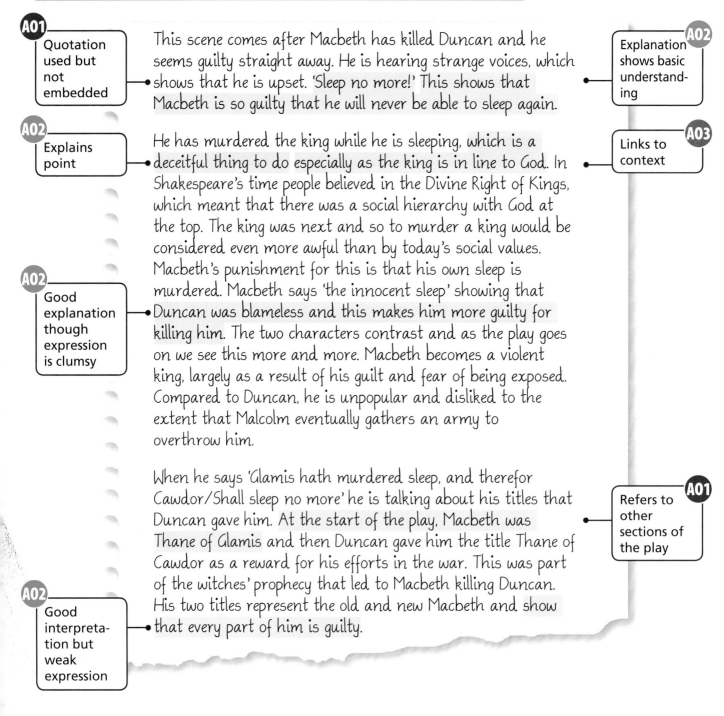

AO1 Quotation used but not embedded

This scene comes after Macbeth has killed Duncan and he seems guilty straight away. He is hearing strange voices, which shows that he is upset. 'Sleep no more!' This shows that Macbeth is so guilty that he will never be able to sleep again.

AO2 Explanation shows basic understanding

AO2 Explains point

He has murdered the king while he is sleeping, which is a deceitful thing to do especially as the king is in line to God. In Shakespeare's time people believed in the Divine Right of Kings, which meant that there was a social hierarchy with God at the top. The king was next and so to murder a king would be considered even more awful than by today's social values. Macbeth's punishment for this is that his own sleep is murdered. Macbeth says 'the innocent sleep' showing that Duncan was blameless and this makes him more guilty for killing him. The two characters contrast and as the play goes on we see this more and more. Macbeth becomes a violent king, largely as a result of his guilt and fear of being exposed. Compared to Duncan, he is unpopular and disliked to the extent that Malcolm eventually gathers an army to overthrow him.

AO3 Links to context

AO2 Good explanation though expression is clumsy

When he says 'Glamis hath murdered sleep, and therefor Cawdor/Shall sleep no more' he is talking about his titles that Duncan gave him. At the start of the play, Macbeth was Thane of Glamis and then Duncan gave him the title Thane of Cawdor as a reward for his efforts in the war. This was part of the witches' prophecy that led to Macbeth killing Duncan. His two titles represent the old and new Macbeth and show that every part of him is guilty.

AO1 Refers to other sections of the play

AO2 Good interpretation but weak expression

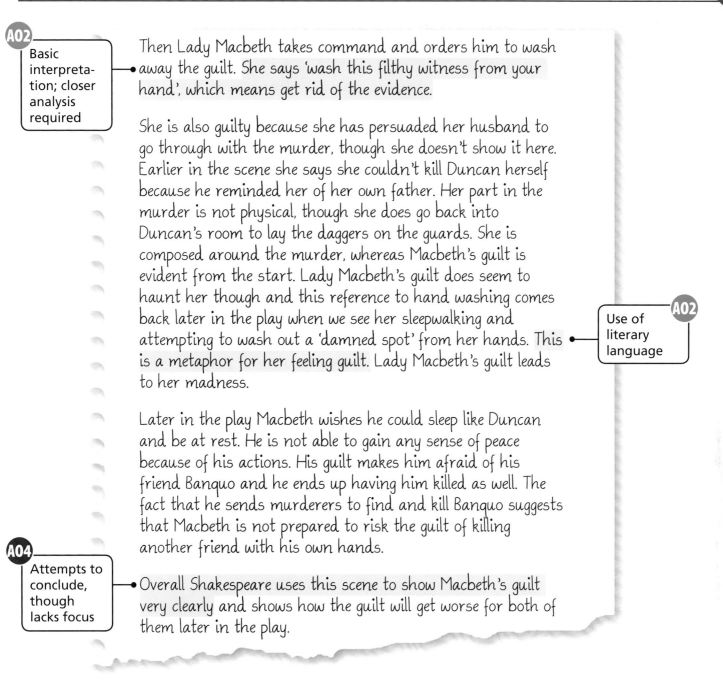

AO2 Basic interpretation; closer analysis required

Then Lady Macbeth takes command and orders him to wash away the guilt. She says 'wash this filthy witness from your hand', which means get rid of the evidence.

She is also guilty because she has persuaded her husband to go through with the murder, though she doesn't show it here. Earlier in the scene she says she couldn't kill Duncan herself because he reminded her of her own father. Her part in the murder is not physical, though she does go back into Duncan's room to lay the daggers on the guards. She is composed around the murder, whereas Macbeth's guilt is evident from the start. Lady Macbeth's guilt does seem to haunt her though and this reference to hand washing comes back later in the play when we see her sleepwalking and attempting to wash out a 'damned spot' from her hands. This is a metaphor for her feeling guilt. Lady Macbeth's guilt leads to her madness.

AO2 Use of literary language

Later in the play Macbeth wishes he could sleep like Duncan and be at rest. He is not able to gain any sense of peace because of his actions. His guilt makes him afraid of his friend Banquo and he ends up having him killed as well. The fact that he sends murderers to find and kill Banquo suggests that Macbeth is not prepared to risk the guilt of killing another friend with his own hands.

AO4 Attempts to conclude, though lacks focus

Overall Shakespeare uses this scene to show Macbeth's guilt very clearly and shows how the guilt will get worse for both of them later in the play.

MID LEVEL

Comment
There are some good points here and the viewpoint is clear, but the style is rather informal. Opportunities for close language analysis are missed and there is a lack of technical vocabulary. There is some very basic reference to historical context.

For a Good Level:
- Develop the points in more detail
- Focus more closely on the effects of language
- Use more sophisticated expression and include technical vocabulary
- Aim for a stronger conclusion
- Include more reference to historical and social context

SAMPLE ANSWER 2

A04 Clear introduction

In this extract Shakespeare shows us how Macbeth is immediately struck with guilty feelings following the murder of Duncan. He thinks he 'heard a voice cry, "Sleep no more!"' This suggests that guilt has resulted in Macbeth hearing voices. It could also imply that he hears his own conscience condemning him for his actions.

A02 Looks at layers of meaning

A04 Uses appropriate technical language

Macbeth refers to 'sleep' repeatedly in this extract. This repetition has the effect of making him seem distracted: he can only think about how he will never sleep again. Sleep is a key motif in the play and will return as evidence of Macbeth's guilt in later scenes. For example in Act III he talks about the 'terrible dreams' (III.2) he is tormented with. This shows how his fears are confirmed and following the murder his guilt prevents him from sleeping.

A01 Shows understanding of play as a whole

A01 Quotation from another section of play

The extent of Macbeth's guilt is due to the fact that, not only has he committed murder, but he has also murdered the king. When Shakespeare wrote the play, society generally believed in the Divine Right of Kings. This meant that the king was directly in line to God. The murder of Duncan is more dreadful because of this. The Macbeths are utterly immoral in their actions and so the guilt they suffer could be interpreted as damnation by God.

A03 Historical context explained

A01 Could expand on this idea

Macbeth is so disturbed that he only carries out part of their plan and forgets to leave the daggers on the guards. This could also show his guilt because he has done the deed and then forgotten what comes next. Lady Macbeth has to take charge and return the daggers herself. At this point in the play she seems more focused on the crime than Macbeth, though we later see the destructive effects of this guilt more visibly in her.

Later when he wants Banquo to be killed, Macbeth doesn't do it himself, but employs murderers to do it. This could be because he knows the lasting effects of guilt and doesn't want to go there again. He wants Banquo's son, Fleance, to be killed as well because he is paranoid about the prophecies.

A02
Begins to explore language

On the other hand, Lady Macbeth seems undisturbed in this extract, and in fact takes charge of the situation. She uses commanding language saying 'Go, get some water' and demanding that her husband clean away 'this filthy witness'. The word 'witness' shows that the blood on Macbeth's hand is visible evidence of his guilt. She takes charge, making her 'brave' husband seem weak. Historically women were considered the weaker sex, yet Lady Macbeth takes control here and is presented as stronger than Macbeth.

A02
Good attention to detail

A03
Good contextual point, could be more developed

A01
Could explore language more closely here

This scene links to the later scene when we see Lady Macbeth's demise. The plan does not work out as she had hoped and her own sleep is upset by her guilt. We see her sleepwalking and making futile attempts to wash a 'damned spot' from her hands. There is irony here as she had previously told her husband that some water would be enough to clean them. The 'spot' represents guilt that cannot be washed out. The Macbeths own knowledge of their crime results in them being 'damned'.

In conclusion, this extract shows some significant examples of guilt that are further developed throughout the play, particularly in the motifs of blood and disturbed sleep.

GOOD LEVEL

Comment
This is a good response that is generally fluent. Evidence is used throughout and technical language is employed to examine the quotations. Reference to the play as a whole is accurate, though sometimes misses opportunities for more detailed connections. More social and historical context required.

For a High Level:
- More reference to wider social and historical context e.g. role of women
- Continue to explore layers of meaning
- Make links to themes
- Comment on overall structure of the play

SAMPLE ANSWER 3

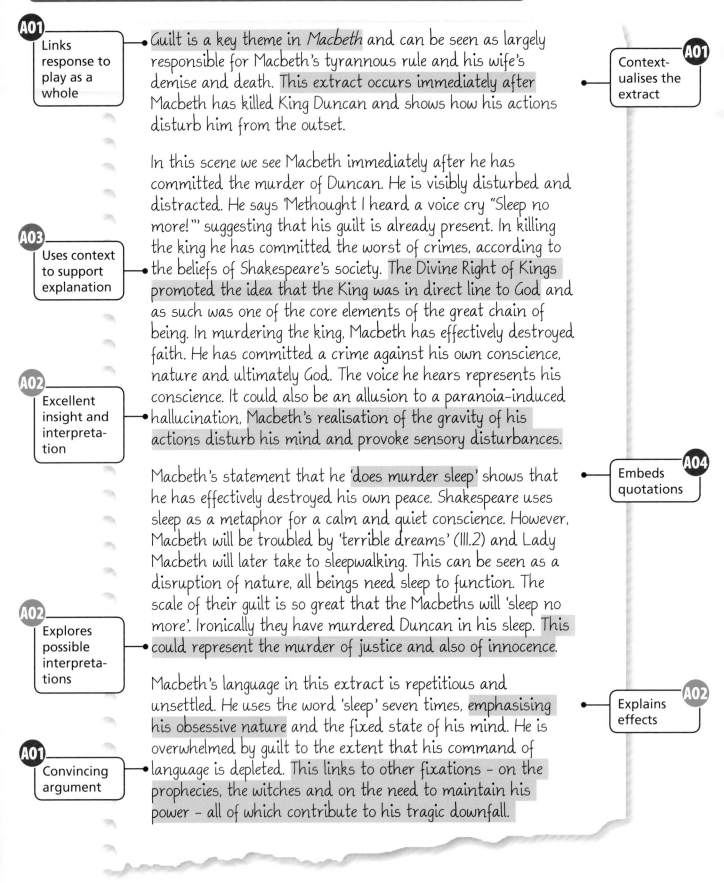

A01 Links response to play as a whole

Guilt is a key theme in *Macbeth* and can be seen as largely responsible for Macbeth's tyrannous rule and his wife's demise and death. This extract occurs immediately after Macbeth has killed King Duncan and shows how his actions disturb him from the outset.

A01 Contextualises the extract

A03 Uses context to support explanation

In this scene we see Macbeth immediately after he has committed the murder of Duncan. He is visibly disturbed and distracted. He says 'Methought I heard a voice cry "Sleep no more!"' suggesting that his guilt is already present. In killing the king he has committed the worst of crimes, according to the beliefs of Shakespeare's society. The Divine Right of Kings promoted the idea that the King was in direct line to God and as such was one of the core elements of the great chain of being. In murdering the king, Macbeth has effectively destroyed faith. He has committed a crime against his own conscience, nature and ultimately God. The voice he hears represents his conscience. It could also be an allusion to a paranoia-induced hallucination, Macbeth's realisation of the gravity of his actions disturb his mind and provoke sensory disturbances.

A02 Excellent insight and interpretation

Macbeth's statement that he 'does murder sleep' shows that he has effectively destroyed his own peace. Shakespeare uses sleep as a metaphor for a calm and quiet conscience. However, Macbeth will be troubled by 'terrible dreams' (III.2) and Lady Macbeth will later take to sleepwalking. This can be seen as a disruption of nature, all beings need sleep to function. The scale of their guilt is so great that the Macbeths will 'sleep no more'. Ironically they have murdered Duncan in his sleep. This could represent the murder of justice and also of innocence.

A04 Embeds quotations

A02 Explores possible interpretations

Macbeth's language in this extract is repetitious and unsettled. He uses the word 'sleep' seven times, emphasising his obsessive nature and the fixed state of his mind. He is overwhelmed by guilt to the extent that his command of language is depleted. This links to other fixations - on the prophecies, the witches and on the need to maintain his power - all of which contribute to his tragic downfall.

A02 Explains effects

A01 Convincing argument

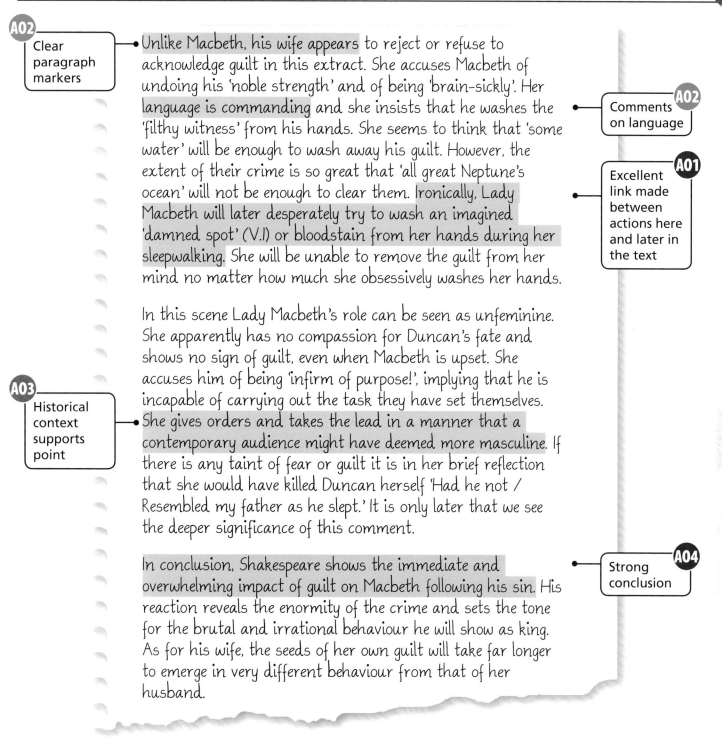

A02
Clear paragraph markers

Unlike Macbeth, his wife appears to reject or refuse to acknowledge guilt in this extract. She accuses Macbeth of undoing his 'noble strength' and of being 'brain-sickly'. Her language is commanding and she insists that he washes the 'filthy witness' from his hands. She seems to think that 'some water' will be enough to wash away his guilt. However, the extent of their crime is so great that 'all great Neptune's ocean' will not be enough to clear them. Ironically, Lady Macbeth will later desperately try to wash an imagined 'damned spot' (V.I) or bloodstain from her hands during her sleepwalking. She will be unable to remove the guilt from her mind no matter how much she obsessively washes her hands.

A02 Comments on language

A01 Excellent link made between actions here and later in the text

A03 Historical context supports point

In this scene Lady Macbeth's role can be seen as unfeminine. She apparently has no compassion for Duncan's fate and shows no sign of guilt, even when Macbeth is upset. She accuses him of being 'infirm of purpose!', implying that he is incapable of carrying out the task they have set themselves. She gives orders and takes the lead in a manner that a contemporary audience might have deemed more masculine. If there is any taint of fear or guilt it is in her brief reflection that she would have killed Duncan herself 'Had he not / Resembled my father as he slept.' It is only later that we see the deeper significance of this comment.

In conclusion, Shakespeare shows the immediate and overwhelming impact of guilt on Macbeth following his sin. His reaction reveals the enormity of the crime and sets the tone for the brutal and irrational behaviour he will show as king. As for his wife, the seeds of her own guilt will take far longer to emerge in very different behaviour from that of her husband.

A04 Strong conclusion

VERY HIGH LEVEL

Comment
A convincing, sustained response that shows excellent understanding and insight. The writing is fluent and well-structured, and technical language is used effortlessly with quotations embedded and fully explored. The inclusion of historical context is relevant and develops the interpretation.

PRACTICE TASK

Write a full-length response to this exam-style question and then use the **Mark scheme** on page 88 to assess your own response.

> **Task:** In Act IV Scene 3, Macduff learns that his wife and children have been murdered.
>
> Read from 'Let not your ears despise my tongue…' to 'the night is long that never finds the day'.
>
> In this extract, how does Shakespeare present Macduff as angry and ready for revenge?
>
> Write about:
> - How Shakespeare presents Macduff in this extract
> - How he is presented in the rest of the play

TOP TIP (A01)

You can use the General skills section of the **Mark scheme** on page 88 to remind you of the key criteria you will need to cover.

Remember:
- Plan quickly and efficiently by using key words from the question
- Write equally about the extract and the rest of the play
- Focus on the techniques Shakespeare uses and the effect of these on the audience
- Support your ideas with relevant evidence, including quotations

FURTHER QUESTIONS

1. Read this extract from Act V Scene 1 in which the doctor observes Lady Macbeth as she sleep walks. It begins 'Lo you, here she comes!' and ends ' … who have died holily in their beds.' Write about how Lady Macbeth is transformed by guilt in this extract. Write about how she is presented in the rest of the play.

2. Read this extract from Act I Scene 3 in which Macbeth and Banquo first meet the witches. It begins 'So foul and fair a day … ' and ends 'Speak, I charge thee!' Write about how Shakespeare presents the theme of the supernatural in this extract and elsewhere in the play.

3. 'The witches are ultimately responsible for the death of King Duncan.' How far do you agree with this view? Explore at least two moments from the play to support your ideas.

4. Explain how Shakespeare explores the theme of ambition in *Macbeth*.

Consider:
- The importance of ambition in the play
- How different characters respond to their ambition

LITERARY TERMS

alliteration	repetition of initial letter in a series of words e.g. 'Fair is foul, and foul is fair'
ambiguity	open to or having several possible meanings or interpretations
aside	a dramatic device in which a character speaks to the audience, unheard by the other characters on stage. It may be addressed to the audience (in character or out) or represent an unspoken thought
blank verse	unrhymed
character(s)	either a person in a play, novel, etc. or his or her personality
choral	when characters speak together – as the witches do in Act I Scene 1
couplet	a pair of rhymed lines of any metre – so verse couplet
dialogue	lines of a play that are spoken by a character
diction	the choice of words in a work of fiction; the kind of vocabulary used
doggerel	bad verse – ill-constructed, rough, clumsy versification
dramatic irony	when the development of the plot allows the audience to possess more information about what is happening than some of the characters themselves have
figurative	any form of expression which deviates from the plainest expression of meaning; language in which words that refer to objects and qualities appeal to the senses and the feelings. Often imagery is expressed through metaphor
foreshadow	a warning of something that will follow later
hyperbole	emphasis by exaggeration
iambic	consisting of the iamb – which is the commonest metrical foot in English verse. It has two syllables, consisting of one weak stress followed by a strong stress, ti-*tum*
iambic pentameter	a line of five iambs
imagery	language that is visually appealing, or creates vivid pictures with words
irony	saying one thing when another is meant
metaphor	a comparison in which one thing is said (or implied) to be another
morality play	the morality plays dealt with good and evil and were particularly popular in Tudor times, though the tradition goes back to medieval times
motif	some aspect of literature (a type of character, theme or image) which recurs frequently
nuance	a subtle difference in or shade of meaning or expression
pathetic fallacy	when setting (often the weather) reflects the mood of a character or scene
pathos	moments in a work of art which evoke strong feelings of pity and sorrow
pentameter	in versification a line of five feet – often iambic
personification	a metaphor in which things or ideas are treated as if they were human beings, with human attributes and feelings
prose	any language that is not patterned by the regularity of metre
protagonist	the main character in a play or narrative
rhyming couplets	pairs of lines with end words that form perfect rhymes
simile	a comparison in which one thing is said to be 'like' or 'as' another
soliloquy	a dramatic convention allowing a character to speak directly to the audience, as if thinking aloud his or her thoughts and feelings
subplot	a story containing minor characters in a play
symbol	something which represents something else, e.g. a rose standing for beauty
theme	the central idea or ideas that the play is about
tragedy	a story that traces the career and downfall of an individual and shows in this downfall both the capacities and limitations of human life. The tragic hero usually has a fatal flaw (in Macbeth's case, ambition) that contributes to his/her downfall
trochaic tetrameter	four feet of stressed-unstressed syllables
verse	poetry, usually with a regular metrical pattern
vocabulary	the choice of words a writer uses

CHECKPOINT ANSWERS

CHECKPOINT 1, page 10

- By asking questions and riddles
- By referring to elemental forces
- By describing their appearance

CHECKPOINT 2, page 12

Because they are saying exactly what he wants to hear and this can only be because they touch a nerve already present in Macbeth.

CHECKPOINT 3, page 13

If Macbeth is to be king, then this is something or someone he must overcome. It appears to trigger in Macbeth a deeper level of plotting and treason.

CHECKPOINT 4, page 16

This is a theme running through the play. Other examples include:

- Lady Macbeth greeting Duncan (I.6)
- Macbeth on learning of Duncan's murder (II.3)
- Macbeth enquiring about Banquo's ride (III.1)
- Macbeth at the banquet for Banquo (III.4)

CHECKPOINT 5, page 18

His openness is in admitting his feelings – which is in stark contrast to Macbeth, who flatly lies that he does not think about the witches.

CHECKPOINT 6, page 21

To prevent discussion of what actually did happen that night. To prevent the guards denying their involvement in Duncan's murder.

CHECKPOINT 7, page 22

Vitally important, despite only appearing in a handful of scenes. Macbeth himself is aware of just how bad he is by contrast with Duncan. Duncan is a touchstone for true kingship and a measure of how a king should be. Set against his standard, Macbeth falls miserably short.

CHECKPOINT 8, page 23

Macbeth's character is degrading as he sinks deeper into evil; he no longer really trusts – or cares about – anybody. As he says in III.4.135–6: 'For mine own good, / All causes shall give way'.

CHECKPOINT 9, page 26

Up until then they may have been prepared to accept Macbeth in the interests of peace, and simply to give him the benefit of the doubt. Now they know they must – and do – act.

CHECKPOINT 10, page 28

The quest for total security is impossible, and in seeking it Macbeth ironically achieves exactly the opposite: for example, Banquo is a threat, but in murdering Banquo most of the other thanes turn against him, thus creating more danger, and less security.

CHECKPOINT 11, page 31

The sense of evil is heightened by: sounds – thunder, music and incantations – as well as sights: the witches, their masters and the apparitions themselves. Macbeth's own dramatic and wicked intentions only add to the sense of urgency of the evil.

CHECKPOINT 12, page 33

He is testing Macduff's integrity because – with all the spies and traitors that Macbeth has created – he is afraid that Macduff might be on Macbeth's side.

CHECKPOINT 13, page 39

Ironically, by his obsessive and literal belief in them. Believing the Wood to be moving, he thinks the prophecy has come true and that he is, therefore, doomed. Because of this, instead of staying in his castle that would 'laugh a siege to scorn' (line 3), he rides out to battle – even though he knows he does not have enough troops to win. Thus, he ensures the prophecy comes true.

PROGRESS AND REVISION CHECK ANSWERS

PART TWO pages 42–3

SECTION ONE

1. Banquo
2. He will become Thane of Cawdor and King
3. Ross
4. By letter
5. The spirits
6. By appealing to his manliness
7. Duncan's chamberlains
8. Sleep
9. Malcolm goes to England, Donalbain to Ireland
10. Macbeth's
11. Three
12. Banquo's
13. 'Eye of newt and toe of frog,/Wool of bat and tongue of dog,/Adder's fork and blind-worm's sting,/Lizard's leg and owlet's wing' (IV.1)
14. Macduff
15. 8
16. Macduff's family
17. On her hands
18. The men use branches as camouflage
19. Seyton
20. Macduff kills him

SECTION TWO

Task 1: Possible ideas:

- The stage direction asks for *'Thunder and lightning'* – **pathetic fallacy** – establishes mood of fear
- Strangeness of the witches – supernatural theme
- Rhyming language and **choral speaking**
- Witches allude to the themes of appearance and reality, evil and justice in their refrain 'Fair is foul and foul is fair' (line 9)

Task 2: Possible ideas:

- Accuses him of cowardice – 'live a coward in thing own esteem' (line 43)
- Challenges his manhood – 'When you durst do it, then you were a man' (line 49)
- Shows her own capacity for violence – 'dashed the brains out' (line 58)
- Shows her determination and conviction of success – 'We fail!' (line 59)

PART THREE page 54

SECTION ONE

1. Duncan is fair; Macbeth is tyrannous
2. Twice
3. She has a breakdown and dies
4. He is murdered on Macbeth's order
5. Macduff
6. Malcolm
7. That they had stayed
8. To England
9. 'Dear Duff'
10. As a ghost

SECTION TWO

Task: Possible ideas:

- He is trusting – is surprised by the treasonous behaviour of original Thane of Cawdor. – 'He was a gentleman on whom I built/An absolute trust' (I.4.15–6)
- He engenders loyalty in his people – 'The service and loyalty I owe,/In doing it, pays itself' (I.4.23–4)
- He is humble and grateful – 'The love that follows us sometime is our trouble' (line 11)
- Duncan's rule is fair and just, unlike Macbeth's – 'this Duncan/Hath borne his faculties so meek' (line 16–7)

PART FOUR page 62

SECTION ONE

1. Ambition
2. Macduff's
3. 'Fair is foul and foul is fair' (I.1.9)
4. King James I
5. The witches
6. Holinshed
7. Four
8. Banquo
9. Donalbain and Malcolm
10. Duncan

Task: Possible ideas:

- After the prophecies, Macbeth sees Malcolm as a threat to his attainment of the throne – 'in my way it lies' (I.4.51)
- Lady Macbeth fears that gentleness will hold her husband back – 'Thou wouldst be great, art not without ambition' (I.5.16–7)
- Macbeth admits ambition is the only reason he has for killing Duncan. 'only/Vaulting ambition' (I.7.26–7)
- Macbeth sends the murderers to kill Banquo and Fleance in protection of his own ambitions. 'Our fears in Banquo/Stick deep' (III.1.49)

PART FIVE page 69

SECTION ONE

1. The Porter, and at times, Lady Macbeth and Lady Macduff
2. Ten
3. Twofold
4. The witches
5. Blood/sleep
6. Acts I and II
7. Tragedy
8. Motif
9. Five
10. Protagonist

SECTION TWO

Task: Possible ideas:

- Macbeth murders Duncan in his sleep – an act of treason and arguably of cowardice. 'Had he not resembled/My father as he slept, I had done't' (II.2.12–13)
- Macbeth fears he will be unable to sleep again after committing his crime – 'Macbeth shall sleep no more' (II.2.43)
- Later Macbeth envies Duncan's sleep of death – 'After life's fitful fever he sleeps well' (III.2.23)
- Lady Macbeth's sleepwalking reveals her troubled mind – 'Here she comes. This is her very guise; and, upon my life, fast asleep.' (V.1.19–20)

MARK SCHEME

POINTS YOU COULD HAVE MADE

- Ross's reluctance to share his news shows that Macduff is likely to respond with anger
- Alliteration of 'Savagely slaughtered' adds to severity
- 'murdered deer' emphasises the innocence of Macduff's family and increases audience sympathy
- Malcolm responds before Macduff, implying that Macduff is shocked into silence
- Macduff's first question 'My children too?' is a partial sentence – this emphasises his distress
- Repetition of 'wife' – shows disbelief
- Malcolm says he must 'dispute it like a man' and Macduff responds decisively
- 'let grief/convert to anger' – Malcolm's imperatives urge Macduff to respond with vengeance
- Macduff calls Macbeth 'this fiend of Scotland' – compares Macbeth to a devil
- 'Macbeth/is ripe for shaking' – metaphor that Macbeth is like a fruit on a tree, ready to be removed

GENERAL SKILLS

Make a judgement about your level based on the points you made (above) and the skills you showed.

Level	Key elements	Spelling, punctuation and grammar	Tick your level
Very high	**Very well-structured answer which gives a rounded and convincing viewpoint.** You use very detailed analysis of the writer's methods and effects on the reader, using precise references which are fluently woven into what you say. You draw inferences, consider more than one perspective or angle, including the context where relevant, and make interpretations about the text as a whole.	You spell and punctuate with consistent accuracy, and use a very wide range of vocabulary and sentence structures to achieve effective control of meaning.	
Good to High	**A thoughtful, detailed response with well-chosen references.** At the top end, you address all aspects of the task in a clearly expressed way, and examine key aspects in detail. You are beginning to consider implications, explore alternative interpretations or ideas; at the top end, you do this fairly regularly and with some confidence.	You spell and punctuate with considerable accuracy, and use a considerable range of vocabulary and sentence structures to achieve general control of meaning.	
Mid	**A consistent response with clear understanding of the main ideas shown.** You use a range of references to support your ideas and your viewpoint is logical and easy to follow. Some evidence of commenting on writers' effects though more needed.	You spell and punctuate with reasonable accuracy, and use a reasonable range of vocabulary and sentence structures.	
Lower	**Some relevant ideas but an inconsistent and rather simple response in places.** You show you have understood the task and you make some points to support what you say, but the evidence is not always well chosen. Your analysis is a bit basic and you do not comment in much detail on the writer's methods.	Your spelling and punctuation is inconsistent and your vocabulary and sentence structures are both limited. Some of these make your meaning unclear.	